"There are three special things that distinguish folks in the South from other people: th[eir] love for good food—their lo[ve] for good friends—and their lo[ve] for a good story."

—John Hagan
This Is What I Love About the South

From Kentucky 'Nanners Foster Waffles to 'Lasses-Glazed Carrots to Sweet Tea and Bourbon Fried Chicken, celebrate the art of *"Country Bling"* cooking with recipes that will have you digging out the cast-iron skillet and running to the store for some butter. Complete with colorful descriptions, accessible ingredients, simple directions, and helpful tips, this book will teach you everything you need to know about cooking with love.

Kentucky born and bred, Lord Honey Chef Jason Smith honors his roots and, at the same time, refashions cherished classics. Enjoy beloved Southern traditions and odes to the homespun—dishes always perfect just the way Granny did it—but with a *twist*. Some of these recipes have won awards, and others haven't made it to the competition yet, but all of them are just right for a sit-down with family and friends.

Lord Honey

Lord Honey

Traditional Southern Recipes

with a
Country Bling Twist

Lord Honey Chef Jason Smith with Lisa Nickell
Photography by Randy Evans
Foreword by Carla Hall

PELICAN PUBLISHING
NEW ORLEANS

The word "Pelican" and the depiction of a pelican are trademarks of Arcadia Publishing Company Inc. and are registered in the U.S. Patent and Trademark Office.

Library of Congress Cataloging-in-Publication Data

Names: Smith, Jason (Lord Honey Chef) author. | Nickell, Lisa, author. | Evans, Randy, 1975- photographer.

Title: Lord Honey: Traditional Southern recipes with a country bling twist / Jason Smith with Lisa Nickell ; photography by Randy Evans; foreword by Carla Hall.

Description: New Orleans : Pelican Publishing, 2023. | Includes index. | Summary: "Lord Honey Chef Jason Smith is a Kentucky native and captivating TV personality who has made it big on Food Network, winning "Holiday Baking Championship," "Holiday Baking Championship-Kids vs Adults," and "Next Food Network Star." In his first cookbook, he has taken his granny's heritage recipes and given them his own twist. From breakfast dishes to lip-smackin', tongue-slappin' sweets, Lord Honey is changing the minds of millions on how traditional food actually looks and tastes"— Provided by publisher.

Identifiers: LCCN 2022034741 | ISBN 9781455626984 (hardcover) | ISBN 9781455626991 (ebook)

Subjects: LCSH: Cooking, American—Southern style. | Cooking—Southern States. | Quick and easy cooking. | LCGFT: Cookbooks.

Classification: LCC TX715.2.S68 S586 2023 | DDC 641.5975—dc23/eng/20220806

LC record available at https://lccn.loc.gov/2022034741

Printed in China
Published by Pelican Publishing
New Orleans, LA
www.pelicanpub.com

*To all the generations of great cooks who have come and gone before me, instillin'
a love for food that has taken me on a tremendous journey, allowin' me to share my
culinary heritage with y'all*

CONTENTS

LORD HONEY

FOREWORD

I am so happy that my dear friend, Jason Smith, is sharing his heritage of food with us. I know that when you read his stories and prepare his recipes, you will feel just like I do—that Jason has the soul of a Southern grandmother that just happens to be wrapped up in a Jason-body and dressed in a sequin jacket. Jason loves people through food. You feel it; you taste it. Jason's sense of family and tradition, along with his sincere approach to staying true to his culinary roots while putting his own touch of love into every dish, will make you feel like you've been wrapped in a warm, cozy blanket on a cold day.

It's evident through his food-competition victories that Jason's recipe for success is sticking to what he knows, and what Jason knows is good Southern-country food. As a Southern cook myself, I feel his passion for sharing his traditions and culture, while passing along his own legacy. Jason knows the importance of sharing tradition through food, and the stories attached to those culinary traditions. He also knows that legacy recipes evolve, with every cook before him having added their own special touch to them before they were ever handed down to him. Just as the family Bible and the family photo album have their additions with each generation, so too do heritage recipes.

It is a blessing that this cookbook will serve as a written record of the traditions and recipes that Jason holds so dear, while at the same time allowing us to get to know him a little better by having a meal with him.

Congratulations, dear friend, in coming full circle, from following the recipes of generations before you to sharing those treasured traditions with all of us.

Carla Hall
cookbook author and international food personality

INTRODUCTION

Lord Honey, for as long as I can remember, my best memories have been made in the kitchen. Cookin' has been my comfort, my inspiration, and my love. I grew up on a farm in Laurel County, Kentucky, learnin' heritage recipes and sharin' in the legacy of homecookin' at my granny's knee.

My love for cookin' didn't stop in Granny's kitchen. The more I cooked, the more I loved it—I just couldn't get enough. It didn't take long for me to realize that food brings people together and makes 'em happy. Family, friends, coworkers, neighbors, and strangers can all have a common experience of enjoyin' a cook's labor. And let me tell y'all, for me, it was, and still is, a labor of love. Honey, if cookin' is a chore, then you ain't been doin' it right.

No matter where I've gone or what jobs I've had, food has been my main passion. It made me happier than a *pig in mud* to see my coworkers' faces light up when I would bring in baked goodies for breakfast and fix lunches, snacks, and dinners to carry us through long workdays. No one seemed to care about the long hours when they knew Ol' Jason was takin' care of the menu.

It seemed a natural path for me to become a caterer on the side of my regular job as a floral designer; I mean, if I was gonna decorate an event, why not just do all the cookin' too? What can I say—I've always been a multitasker. Let me tell y'all, I stayed *as busy as a one-toothed beaver buildin' a dam.*

Through the years, I have taken time-proven, classic recipes and updated 'em by addin' my own special touches. I developed a style I like to call *"Country Bling."* It is this style that helped me win three Food Network competitions within a year's time: *Holiday Baking Championship,* season 3; *Holiday Baking Championship, Kids vs. Adults* 2016; and *Food Network Star,* season 13.

While comin' up with my *"Country Bling"* makeovers, I have tried very hard to stay true to my Southern roots and my Kentucky heritage—usin' what I call the *"Southern Trinity"* of Bacon, Butter, & Bourbon.

Along with the *"Trinity,"* I have added fresh, vibrant ingredients and new approaches to traditional Southern comfort foods, maintainin' the rich, comfortin' flavors that once took hours to develop. Let's face it, ever'one has such hectic schedules nowadays that it is almost impossible to prepare a meal the way the generations before us did. I hope, by bringin' new ways to enjoy these recipes, that the legacy of our ancestors' homecookin' will not disappear.

Some of my most cherished items are the handwritten recipes and antique cookbooks from my granny and aunts, who are no longer with me. I consider these recipes and books to be a type of folklore, and I feel a responsibility to make sure they continue to be passed down. I love the memories that come floodin' back when I make and share some of my favorite childhood recipes. Even though I've put my own *twists* on some of these tried-and-true classics, it is important to preserve the original recipes as part of my history.

Over the years, when I shared my updated traditional dishes, people asked me for my recipes. I would write 'em down or make copies of 'em to share. All along, my family, friends, and fans encouraged me to put my *"Country Bling"* creations into a cookbook. I will admit that a cookbook was always at the top of my bucket list.

One of my absolute favorite things about cookbooks is the idea that they let people, hundreds or thousands of miles apart, from farms to cities, North to South, East to West, prepare the same recipe and share the same food, possibly even on the same day. Now ain't that just the *neatest thing since puttin' a pocket on a shirt?*

Whether old or new, cookbooks are about recordin' and preservin' a part of our culture, servin' as a roadmap to the past, present, and future of our food traditions and customs.

Along with *twisted* traditional Southern dishes, such as sweet tater casserole, fried chicken, okra, and peach cobbler, I have included my *twisted* versions of recipes unique to my home state of Kentucky, such as the famous Hot Brown sandwich, beer cheese, and Kentucky butter cake. It goes without sayin' that I've added bourbon to a lot of recipes, to give 'em a Kentucky *twist*.

I hope y'all have a *hootin'-hollerin'* good time cookin' and eatin' my *twisted* recipes with your kith-n-kin.

My greatest wish is that, just as I have cherished all the cookbooks and recipes that have been handed down to me, *Lord Honey: Traditional Southern Recipes with a Country Bling Twist* will become a lasting tradition in your home and family.

Enjoy!

Lord Honey

Chapter 1

ROOSTER'S CROWIN' (BREAKFAST)

Apple Hoecakes with Bourbon Syrup

Blackberry Crunch Muffins

Blueberry-Zucchini Skillet Bread

Breakfast Cobbler

Breakfast Rice with Berries

Brown Sugar-Walnut Fried Apples

Cherry Cobbler Coffeecake

Country Ham and Redeye Gravy

Farmhouse Skillet

Fruity French Toast Stack

Grits and Gouda Breakfast Casserole

Hot Brown Breakfast Quiche

Just Peachy Sticky Buns

Kentucky 'Nanners Foster Waffles

Maple Bacon Goodies

New Country Sawmill Sausage Gravy

Southern-Best Butter Biscuit

Southern-Best Bacon and Butter Biscuit

Southern Honey Biscuit with
Bourbon-Coffee Glaze

Sweet and Savory Bread Puddin'

Sweet Tater Fritters

Tasty Tater Casserole

Growin' up on a farm in Kentucky, we would rise and shine with the rooster's crow. Everyone had early-mornin' chores to do, either on the farm or in the kitchen. I always went to the kitchen with Granny and helped her with the chore of makin' sure that everyone had a full belly before startin' a long day on the farm. Let me tell y'all, we were *busier than an 18-hour bra on a 24-hour shift.*

No matter what was on Granny's breakfast table, I can guarantee you one thing, there was always biscuits and gravy. It's an unwritten rule of the South: it just ain't breakfast without it. We love our biscuits and gravy so much that sometimes we even have it for supper.

Whether y'all want a full breakfast spread, a little bite with your mornin' coffee, or a tasty brunch dish, I hope you enjoy the *twists* on some of my favorite breakfast recipes.

Apple Hoecakes with Bourbon Syrup

What wonderful memories I have of my grandmother's hoecakes and fried apples for breakfast. I've taken this nostalgic duo and given it a li'l twist with some yummy bourbon syrup. I'm not sure this would get Granny's stamp of approval, but I know it's always a hit when I serve it for breakfast or brunch.

Serves 6-8

INGREDIENTS:
1 cup self-rising white or yellow cornmeal
1 cup self-rising flour
3 tbsp. white sugar
3 tbsp. light brown sugar
1 tsp. ground cinnamon
⅛ tsp. ground cloves
1 cup full-fat buttermilk
1 tsp. vanilla
2 eggs
¼ cup canola oil
1 large Golden Delicious apple, peeled and chopped

Add 1 tsp. bourbon to the batter for an extra kick.

SYRUP:
2 cups maple syrup
3 tbsp. butter, melted
3 tbsp. bourbon
1 tsp. ground nutmeg

GARNISH:
Butter
Chopped pecans
Powdered sugar

DIRECTIONS:
- In a medium mixing bowl, whisk together the cornmeal, flour, white and brown sugar, cinnamon, and cloves.

- Add the buttermilk, vanilla, eggs, and oil, and stir to combine.

- Fold in the apples.

- Heat griddle to medium, and pour batter into small cakes (¼ cup each) on the hot griddle. Let cook until brown on bottom, flip, and brown second side. This takes about 3-4 minutes per side.

- Place on a serving platter and dot with butter. Repeat frying until all batter is gone.

- Place the syrup ingredients in a quart-sized mason jar, put on lid, and shake until combined.

- Pour desired amounts of syrup on hoecakes, and garnish with pecans and powdered sugar.

Blackberry Crunch Muffins

Y'all know I love to share things from my home state of Kentucky, so I just had to include our state berry—the blackberry. Enjoy my twist on coffeecake and muffins, with a savory cinnamon crunch and the sweet, tart pop of fresh blackberries.

Serves 12

INGREDIENTS:

2¼ cups self-rising flour
1 cup white sugar
¼ cup brown sugar
½ cup canola oil
2 eggs
2 tsp. vanilla
¾ cup full-fat buttermilk
1½ cups fresh or frozen blackberries
Zest of 1 lime

To get all the juice from citrus, microwave the fruit for 10 seconds, then juice.

CRUNCH TOPPING:

½ cup white sugar
¼ cup brown sugar, packed
½ cup self-rising flour
½ cup quick-cook oats
¼ cup sweetened shredded coconut
½ cup chopped walnuts
5 tbsp. butter, room temp
1 tsp. ground cinnamon
½ tsp. ground ginger

GLAZE:

2 cups powdered sugar
½ tsp. salt
1 tsp. vanilla
Juice of 1 lime

DIRECTIONS:

- Preheat oven to 375 degrees. Grease or line a 12-hole muffin tin.

- In a mixing bowl, whisk together the flour and sugars. Add the oil, eggs, vanilla, and buttermilk, and stir to combine.

- In a small bowl, toss the blackberries with 1 tbsp. flour, then add the berries and zest to the batter and lightly fold them in.

- Place the crunch topping ingredients in a bowl and mix with a fork until large crumbles form.

- Divide the batter evenly into the muffin tin, and sprinkle tops with crunch mixture.

- Bake for 22-28 minutes or until a toothpick comes out clean.

- Remove from oven and place on cooling rack.

- Place the glaze ingredients in a bowl and whisk until combined. Drizzle over cooled muffins.

Blueberry-Zucchini Skillet Bread

Zucchini is one of those garden treats that just keeps givin'—all summer long. I mean, how much loaf bread can a person eat? Well, I've put my twist on the traditional zucchini loaf by addin' a zing of ginger and a fresh pop of blueberry and throwin' it all in an iron skillet.

Makes 2 10-inch skillets

INGREDIENTS:
Nonstick cooking spray
1¾ cups white sugar
¼ cup brown sugar, packed
1 cup veggie oil
3 eggs
2 tsp. vanilla
1 tsp. ground cinnamon
¾ tsp. ground ginger, or 1 tsp. grated fresh ginger
2 cups grated zucchini
3 cups self-rising flour
1½ cups fresh blueberries

When working with fresh berries in baked goods, remember always to toss them with a little flour before adding to the batter. This keeps them from sinking to the bottom during baking.

LEMON GLAZE:
3 cups powdered sugar
1 tbsp. milk
2 tbsp. lemon juice
¼ cup butter, melted
Zest of 1 lemon

GARNISH:
Sliced lemons
Fresh blueberries

DIRECTIONS:
- Preheat oven to 350 degrees and spray 2 10-inch cast-iron skillets with nonstick cooking spray.
- Cream the sugars and oil together in a mixing bowl.
- Add eggs, vanilla, cinnamon, and ginger, and stir to combine.
- Stir in the zucchini.
- Add the flour and mix just until combined.
- In a small bowl, toss the blueberries with 1 tbsp. flour, then lightly stir into the batter, making sure not to crush them.
- Divide the batter between the skillets.
- Bake for 45-60 minutes or until a toothpick comes out clean.
- Remove from oven and let cool before glazing.
- Place the glaze ingredients in a mixing bowl and stir until combined.
- Spread over breads.
- Garnish with sliced lemons and fresh blueberries.

Breakfast Cobbler

Cobblers are as Southern as Southern gets, but you usually don't think of 'em for breakfast. Well, honey, I've taken the idea of the cobbler and given it a savory twist, with the comfortin' flavors of a full-course breakfast—all in one yummy cheese-covered dish.

Serves 8

INGREDIENTS:

Nonstick cooking spray
1 lb. sage breakfast sausage
8 eggs
1 cup half-and-half
¼ cup chopped green onions
½ tsp. salt
1 tsp. onion powder
¼ tsp. ground black pepper
¼ tsp. garlic powder
½ tsp. crushed red pepper flakes
12 frozen biscuits, thawed and quartered
2½ cups shredded mild cheddar cheese
4 tbsp. butter, melted

This is good made with ham or bacon instead of sausage.

DIRECTIONS:

- Preheat oven to 375 degrees and spray a 9x13 baking dish with nonstick cooking spray.

- Cook and crumble the sausage. Drain on a paper-towel-lined plate.

- In a medium bowl, mix the eggs, half-and-half, onions, and spices.

- Place the biscuits in the bottom of prepared dish, making a single layer. Sprinkle half the cheese over biscuits, then the sausage and rest of cheese.

- Pour the egg mixture over all.

- Drizzle the butter over top.

- Bake for 30-35 minutes, or until the biscuits are puffed and golden brown.

- Once baked, let stand for 10 minutes before serving.

Breakfast Rice with Berries

I grew up eatin' rice for breakfast, the same as oatmeal—a li'l sugar, butter, and milk. I never knew you ate it any other time, and now folks rarely think of rice as a breakfast dish. Well, hopefully my twist on this old-time favorite will lead to the revival of rice for breakfast. With its sweet, crunchy, fresh berry toppin', I just know y'all will be addin' this to your list of breakfast favorites.

Serves 4

INGREDIENTS:

2 cups water
8 tbsp. butter, divided
½ tsp. salt
1 cup rice
2 tbsp. heavy cream

BERRY TOPPING:

1 cup fresh blueberries
½ cup fresh raspberries
1 cup sliced fresh strawberries
½ cup pecan halves
½ cup honey

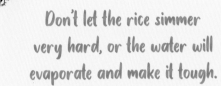

Don't let the rice simmer very hard, or the water will evaporate and make it tough.

DIRECTIONS:

- In a medium saucepan over medium heat, bring the water to a boil.
- Add 4 tbsp. butter and the salt, and let butter melt. Return to a boil. Add the rice and stir.
- Put lid on pot and turn to simmer.
- Let simmer for 17-25 minutes—no longer. Check a few times to make sure it's not simmering too hard.
- Take off burner and let stand with lid on for 5 minutes.
- Remove lid and fluff with fork. Add the heavy cream and the rest of the butter, and stir.
- Place the rice in a serving bowl and top with fruit and nuts. Drizzle with honey.

Brown Sugar-Walnut Fried Apples

Two things we always knew we would have an abundance of in the fall was apples and walnuts. We had apples, one way or another, at every meal, and Granny mostly used the walnuts for bakin' and candy-makin'. I liked to put walnuts in my fried apples to give 'em a li'l crunch. Needless to say, Granny thought I was wastin' perfectly good walnuts. It wasn't much of a stretch to know how I wanted to put a twist on traditional fried apples—a whole lot of sweetness, a bit of spice, and, of course, the crunchy bite of walnuts.

Serves 6

INGREDIENTS:
5 tbsp. butter
6 apples, peeled, cored, and sliced
4 tbsp. white sugar
½ cup dark brown sugar, packed
Pinch of salt
2 tsp. ground cinnamon
1 tsp. ground nutmeg
1 cup walnuts, chopped

You want apples that don't break down too much during cooking, such as Granny Smith, Braeburn, or Golden Delicious.

DIRECTIONS:

- In a large skillet over medium heat, melt the butter. Add the apples, sugars, salt, and spices; stir to combine. Cook for 6-8 minutes. Place lid on skillet and turn to low.

- Let apples cook until fork tender but not mushy. Transfer to serving dish and top with nuts.

Cherry Cobbler Coffeecake

Cherries was somethin' we didn't have much of growin' up, so whenever we got to eat a cherry pie or cherry cobbler, it was a special day. Coffeecake wasn't eaten for breakfast or dessert but as an occasional afternoon snack for the adults. I would always try to sneak a bite before they ate it all up. So, I thought I would do a twist on two special treats from my childhood: sweet and tart cherry cobbler with all the warm flavors and crunch of coffeecake.

Serves 12

INGREDIENTS:

2 cups self-rising flour
1 cup white sugar
½ cup canola oil
1 cup buttermilk or whole milk
2 eggs
2 tsp. vanilla
1 tsp. almond extract
1 (16 oz.) bag frozen dark sweet cherries, thawed
1 (10 oz.) jar maraschino cherries, cut in half

CRUMB TOPPING:

¼ cup flour
¼ cup light brown sugar
½ tsp. salt
¼ cup old-fashioned oats
5 tbsp. butter, cubed and cold
½ cup sliced almonds

GLAZE:

3 cups powdered sugar
1 tbsp. butter, melted
2 tsp. vanilla
2 tbsp. milk
1 tsp. maraschino cherry juice

GARNISH:

Sliced or slivered almonds
Maraschino cherries
Fresh or frozen cherries

> When working with butter for a crumb topping, it's super important to make sure it is very cold.

DIRECTIONS:

- Preheat oven to 350 degrees. Grease a 12-inch round cake pan.

- In a large mixing bowl, mix the flour, sugar, oil, buttermilk, eggs, vanilla, and almond extract until smooth. Batter will be thick.

- Pour the batter into prepared cake pan, and top batter with the cherries.

- Bake for 60-75 minutes, or until golden brown and a toothpick comes out clean.

- Make the crumb topping by placing the flour, sugar, salt, and oats in a bowl. Add the butter and cut in with a fork until large crumbles form. Stir in almonds and set aside.

- Halfway through baking, remove pan and sprinkle on crumb topping. Return to oven and finish baking.

- Remove from oven and let cool for 45 minutes, then take out of pan and place on serving plate.
- Place the glaze ingredients in a mixing bowl and whisk together. Drizzle over the cake.
- Garnish with nuts and cherries.

Country Ham and Redeye Gravy

Children, I know I bombard y'all with a lot of Southern dishes—and a lot of 'em you've probably eaten at some time or other. Well, here's one not all Southerners have tried: redeye gravy. Believe me when I tell y'all that country ham and redeye gravy is as Southern as it gets. It's so perfectly Southern that even I won't give it a twist. If you're not wide-eyed and wooly before you eat it, you most definitely will be after.

Serves 6

INGREDIENTS:
2 tbsp. canola oil
1 (12 oz.) pkg. country ham
¾ cup brewed coffee
¾ cup water
1 tsp. ground black pepper

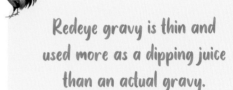

Redeye gravy is thin and used more as a dipping juice than an actual gravy.

DIRECTIONS:
- Heat the oil in a large skillet over medium heat.
- Trim the ham into smaller pieces. Place in the hot skillet and fry for about 2 minutes per side, making sure to get caramelization on both sides. Transfer to a serving platter.
- Pour coffee into the hot skillet and scrape the bits of ham off the bottom. Add the water and bring to a boil. Allow the liquid to reduce for about 5-6 minutes, then add the pepper.
- Pour into a serving bowl.

Farmhouse Skillet

This dish is based on an old breakfast casserole that we used to call "Its & Bits." That meant we threw together whatever we had to make a tasty breakfast treat, so it was a surprise ever'time. I've given it a twist by adding fresh vegetables to all my favorite breakfast foods. Y'all can add to or take away from this recipe and use your favorite "Its & Bits" to make it your own breakfast surprise.

Serves 8-10

INGREDIENTS:

1 lb. bacon, diced
2 cups cubed cooked ham
1/2 lb. breakfast sausage, cooked and crumbled
1 small purple onion, diced
1/2 red bell pepper, diced
1/2 yellow bell pepper, diced
10 eggs, beaten
1/2 cup heavy cream
1 (20 oz.) pkg. frozen shredded hash browns, or tater tots, thawed
Salt and ground black pepper to taste
1 cup shredded Monterey Jack cheese

This makes a great brunch dish.

DIRECTIONS:

· Preheat oven to 350 degrees.

· In a very large cast-iron skillet (12-inch or larger), over medium heat, cook the bacon until crispy. Then add the ham and sausage and stir.

· Add the onions and peppers, and sauté for 5 minutes, always stirring.

· In a small bowl, whisk the eggs and heavy cream.

· Stir the hash browns into the skillet, and add salt and pepper to taste. Cook for 5-8 minutes, until hash browns start to brown. Remove from heat. Add the egg mixture, top with cheese, and bake for 20-25 minutes or until bubbly and cheese is melted.

Fruity French Toast Stack

French toast is my mom's favorite breakfast meal. She also loves fruit and honey when she wants somethin' light. So why not put 'em together, so she can have the best of both worlds? Well, that's exactly what this twist does. It takes the comfort of a nice, hot, golden French toast stick and adds the sweet freshness of berries and honey.

Serves 4

INGREDIENTS:
2 pkg. fresh blackberries
2 pkg. fresh raspberries
2 pkg. fresh strawberries, capped and halved
½ cup honey
Zest and juice of 1 orange
2 pkg. frozen French toast sticks

GARNISH:
Sweetened whipped cream
Fresh mint
Orange slices

If you can't find fresh berries, use frozen, but let them thaw first.

DIRECTIONS:
- Preheat a waffle iron.

- Wash and drain berries, and place in a bowl.

- Add the honey, orange zest, and juice to berries and toss to coat.

- Place 8 toast sticks in waffle iron and mash lid down. Cook until light brown. Remove and keep cooking the remaining sticks until they are all cooked.

- Place sticks on serving plates, stacking them up in a crisscross pattern.

- Spoon fruit over top, and garnish with whipped cream, mint, and orange slices.

Grits and Gouda Breakfast Casserole

What are a Southerner's favorite words when ordering breakfast, lunch, or dinner? Well, I'm gonna tell y'all: Grits! Grits! Grits! That's right, grits in the mornin', grits in the daytime, grits at suppertime. Hey, I think I have a new song. I do know one thing for sure—y'all will be singin' like a robin in the springtime when you get a mouthful of my twist on old-fashioned grits and cheese.

Serves 6-8

INGREDIENTS:

2 cups water
3 cups veggie stock
1 cup canned evaporated milk
2 tsp. salt
1 tsp. ground black pepper
½ tsp. garlic powder
½ tsp. onion powder
½ tsp. cayenne pepper (optional)
2 cups quick-cook grits
1 lb. sage breakfast sausage, cooked and crumbled
3 eggs
6 tbsp. butter, melted
3 cups shredded smoked gouda

GARNISH:

Chopped parsley
Sprigs of sage

Grits come in white or yellow. Either one will work for this recipe.

DIRECTIONS:

- Preheat oven to 350 degrees. Butter an 11x7 casserole dish and set aside.

- In a large pot, bring water, stock, and cream to a low boil.

- Add salt, pepper, garlic powder, onion powder, and cayenne pepper. Stir. Slowly pour in grits. Turn heat down to low and cook for 5 minutes, stirring to make sure grits do not stick. Remove pot from stove and let grits cool for 8-10 minutes.

- Stir in the cooked sausage.

- In a bowl, mix the eggs and butter.

- Add the egg mixture and cheese to the grits and stir to combine.

- Pour into prepared dish and bake for 50 minutes, until the center is set and the top is golden brown.

- Remove from oven and let set for 10 minutes. Sprinkle with chopped parsley and sprigs of sage.

Hot Brown Breakfast Quiche

For anyone who doesn't know, the Hot Brown is a signature sandwich from the state of Kentucky. It was created at the Brown Hotel in Louisville in 1926. It has been adored and worshipped ever since as the perfect dish to serve for brunch or lunch. I have taken the key ingredients of this esteemed sandwich and given it a twist. This breakfast quiche features all the wonderful flavors that make the Hot Brown so near and dear to every Kentuckian's heart.

Serves 6

INGREDIENTS:
Nonstick cooking spray
1 prepared pie dough sheet
1½ cups diced cooked turkey
1½ cups shredded white cheddar cheese
⅔ cup crumbled cooked bacon
½ cup diced tomatoes
3 eggs
1 cup half-and-half
3 tbsp. sour cream
1 tsp. onion powder
½ tsp. salt
1 tsp. ground black pepper

GARNISH:
Cooked bacon strips
Diced tomatoes

DIRECTIONS:
- Preheat oven to 350 degrees. Spray a 9-inch pie plate with nonstick cooking spray. Place the dough in pie plate, and crimp edges.

- Spread the turkey, cheese, bacon, and tomatoes in bottom of pie shell.

- Whisk together the eggs, half-and-half, sour cream, onion powder, salt, and pepper.

- Pour over ingredients in pie shell.

- Bake for 1 hour. Remove from oven and let rest for 10 minutes before serving.

- Garnish with more cooked bacon and diced tomatoes.

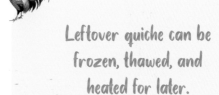

Leftover quiche can be frozen, thawed, and heated for later.

Just Peachy Sticky Buns

Sticky buns are a classic when it comes to breakfast pastries. Well, y'all know by now that I like to give the classic a li'l twist. I've done just that by replacing traditional dough with puff pastry and adding the sweetness of peaches and the crunch of cashews. When y'all serve this to your guests, they won't want to leave; they will just keep stickin' around.

Serves 12

INGREDIENTS:
Nonstick cooking spray
8 oz. cream cheese, softened
1 cup packed light brown sugar, divided
1 tsp. vanilla
$\frac{1}{2}$ tsp. ground ginger
$\frac{1}{2}$ tsp. ground nutmeg
2 sheets store-bought puff pastry, room temp
2 (15 oz.) cans diced peaches, drained, juice reserved for glaze
$\frac{1}{2}$ cup butter, melted
$1\frac{1}{2}$ cups cashews, whole or pieces

This can be made with any canned fruit.

GLAZE:
3 cups powdered sugar
2 tsp. vanilla
2-3 tbsp. reserved peach juice

GARNISH:
Cashews
Fresh sliced peaches
Fresh whipped cream

DIRECTIONS:
- Preheat oven to 400 degrees and spray a 9x13 baking dish with nonstick cooking spray.

- In a small mixing bowl, mix together the cream cheese, half the brown sugar, the vanilla, ginger, and nutmeg.

- Place the puff pastry flat on a piece of parchment paper. Spread half of the cream cheese mixture on each sheet of dough. Sprinkle the drained peaches evenly over the cream cheese layer on both pieces. From the short end, roll dough up into a log. Slice each roll into 6 pieces.

- Spread the melted butter evenly in the bottom of the baking dish. Sprinkle with the remaining brown sugar and the cashews.

- Place the 12 rolls, flat side down, on top of the nuts.

- Bake for 30-35 minutes or until golden brown.

- While the rolls are baking, place the glaze ingredients in a bowl and whisk together. The glaze should not be very runny.

- When buns are baked, remove from oven and let rest for 5 minutes. Then invert onto a serving platter and let cool for 30-40 minutes.

- Spoon the glaze over buns.

- Garnish with more nuts and sliced peaches, and serve with whipped cream.

Kentucky 'Nanners Foster Waffles

A traditional Bananas Foster is a very sweet dessert made with rum and served with ice cream. So how do you twist it into a Kentucky breakfast dish? Why, add bourbon and serve it over waffles, of course! Get ready to be left speechless by the pure decadence of this twisted dish.

Serves 4-6

INGREDIENTS:

Nonstick cooking spray
2 cups all-purpose flour
¼ cup white sugar
1 tbsp. baking powder
1 tsp. salt
2 eggs
1½ cups milk, any variety
½ cup butter, melted and cooled
2 tsp. vanilla
½ tsp. ground cinnamon

TOPPING:

¼ cup butter
¼ cup brown sugar, packed
¼ tsp. ground cinnamon
¼ tsp. ground nutmeg
2 bananas, sliced thick
3 tbsp. bourbon
Favorite vanilla ice cream

Feel free to use apple juice in place of the bourbon.

DIRECTIONS:

- Preheat a waffle iron, and spray with nonstick cooking spray. Preheat oven to 170 degrees.

- In a large bowl, whisk together the flour, sugar, baking powder, and salt.

- In a small bowl, whisk the eggs and milk. Add the butter, vanilla, and cinnamon, and whisk.

- Add the wet mixture to the dry, and whisk until there are no lumps.

- Scoop ½ cup batter onto the waffle iron, close the lid, and let cook until golden brown and crispy. Repeat until all batter is gone.

- Put the waffles on a sheet pan and place in preheated oven.

- To make the topping, melt the butter in a medium skillet over medium heat. Add the brown sugar, cinnamon, and nutmeg, stir to combine, and cook for about 1 minute.

- Add the sliced bananas and cook for a few seconds. Add the bourbon, and cook 2-3 minutes, stirring often with a light hand so the bananas do not break up.

- Meanwhile, place 1-2 waffles on a plate and top with a scoop of ice cream. Once banana sauce has thickened, spoon over ice cream and waffles. Repeat with remaining waffles.

Maple Bacon Goodies

My aunt Brenda loves maple goodies candy, so I wanted to come up with a twist that would give her all the flavor of her favorite candy in a breakfast dish. Y'all know me—add bacon to anything and you can call it breakfast.

Makes 1 dozen

INGREDIENTS:
8 strips bacon, cubed
1 can crescent roll dough
¼ cup butter
¼ cup maple syrup
¾ cup brown sugar
⅓ cup chopped pecans, toasted (see tip)

> When working with nuts, always toast them first in a skillet over medium heat, tossing them until they give off a toasty aroma. Be careful not to scorch them.

DIRECTIONS:

- Preheat oven to 375 degrees. Grease a sheet pan.

- In a skillet, cook bacon until crispy. Drain and reserve the drippings.

- Place the crescent roll dough on prepared sheet pan, making sure it's a flat sheet. Prick all over with a fork.

- Melt the butter, and stir in the bacon drippings.

- Brush the maple syrup over dough.

- Sprinkle with brown sugar, then sprinkle with the pecans and cooked bacon.

- Drizzle the butter mixture over top.

- Bake for 20-25 minutes.

- Remove from oven, cut into 12 squares, and transfer to a serving platter. Serve warm or room temp.

New Country Sawmill Sausage Gravy

"Sawmill" is a southern Appalachian way of sayin' white breakfast gravy made with fat drippin's. Now some folks like their sausage on the side, and some like it cooked in the gravy. Another gravy debate is whether you ladle it over split biscuits or torn biscuits. I just say, no matter what twist y'all wanna give it, it's gravy, baby.

Serves 6-8

INGREDIENTS:

1 lb. breakfast sausage
½ cup flour
1½ cups milk
½ cup water
½ tsp. ground black pepper
¼ tsp. salt
¼ tsp. onion powder

If you do not want to use sausage, substitute ¼ cup bacon drippings or canola oil.

DIRECTIONS:

- In a large skillet over medium heat, cook and crumble sausage until done.

- Add the flour to the sausage, frying for 3-4 minutes.

- Pour in the milk and stir until the gravy starts to thicken. Then add the water, and stir.

- Sprinkle in the pepper, salt, and onion powder. Taste for seasoning, and adjust to your liking.

- Serve with warm biscuits, bacon, or sausage or with fried chicken and cornbread.

"BUTTER MY BUTT AND CALL ME A BISCUIT"

In the South, we call a big ol' made-from-scratch biscuit a "cathead" biscuit, because we make 'em as big as a cat's head. Don't ask me how this started or why it's not a hog-head or a possum-head—I ain't gotta clue. I just know there's nothin' better than a hot, golden-brown, flaky, fluffy "cathead" biscuit. We eat biscuits at ever' meal, enjoy them as snacks, and even use 'em in our desserts. It's not hard to figure out that biscuits are the South's bread of choice. I'm givin' y'all the "Southern Trinity" of biscuits: a versatile, rich, buttery one; a savory one bustin' with bacon; and a sweet one with a bourbon glaze to enjoy with your mornin' coffee.

Southern-Best Butter Biscuit

Makes 1 dozen

INGREDIENTS:
4 cups self-rising flour
1 tbsp. baking powder
1 tbsp. white sugar
1½ sticks butter, frozen and grated
2 cups buttermilk
2 tbsp. butter, melted, for topping

An iron skillet is an excellent pan to use when making biscuits.

DIRECTIONS:
- Preheat oven to 400 degrees. Grease a baking sheet.
- In a large mixing bowl, whisk together the flour, baking powder, and sugar.
- Fold in the grated butter, using a light hand.
- Make a well in the middle of the flour mixture. Pour the buttermilk into the well, and fold the flour into the milk gently until the dough forms a ball.
- Place the dough on a floured surface and pat until it is ¾ inch thick.
- Fold dough in half. Pat again until it is ¾ inch thick. Repeat 2 more times.
- Once your final pat is ¾ inch thick, use a biscuit cutter dipped into flour to cut into rounds. Dip the cutter into flour frequently to keep the dough from sticking to it.
- Place on prepared baking sheet, making sure the biscuits touch—this helps them to rise.
- Brush with melted butter.
- Bake about 25-30 minutes, until golden brown.

Southern-Best Bacon and Butter Biscuit

Remember, bacon makes ever'thing better.

You can use dried fruits or fresh herbs to have a variety of sweet and savory biscuits.

DIRECTIONS:
- Follow my Southern-Best Butter Biscuit recipe (see index), adding 10 slices cooked, crispy, crumbled bacon to the dough mixture.

Southern Honey Biscuit with Bourbon-Coffee Glaze

My granny used to make me a breakfast treat she called "Soak Ups," a small saucer filled with coffee, cream, and sugar, with a warm, fluffy biscuit set right in the middle of it. Oh, how I loved taking my spoon and digging into that warm biscuit soaked in that sweet coffee. This twist honors all the flavors–except for bourbon, of course–that my granny made special for me.

Makes 1 dozen

INGREDIENTS:
3 cups all-purpose flour
1 tbsp. baking powder
½ tsp. baking soda
1 tsp. salt
1 cup whole milk
¼ cup honey
½ tsp. vanilla bean paste or vanilla extract
¾ cup butter, frozen and grated
¼ cup buttermilk, for topping
3 tbsp. light brown sugar, for topping

BOURBON-COFFEE GLAZE:
1 tbsp. bourbon
2 tbsp. water
1 tbsp. instant coffee granules
2½ cups powdered sugar

Instead of bourbon, you can add your favorite flavor of liquid coffee creamer.

DIRECTIONS:
- Preheat oven to 400 degrees. Line a baking sheet with parchment paper.

- In a mixing bowl, whisk the flour, baking powder, baking soda, and salt to combine.
- In a small bowl, add the milk, honey, and vanilla, and stir to mix.
- Add the frozen butter to the flour, and toss with a very light hand until it looks like crumbly cornmeal.
- Put in the fridge for 15 minutes to allow butter to set.
- Remove flour mixture from fridge and make a well in the middle. Pour the milk mixture into the well, and fold the flour into the milk gently, until the dough forms a ball.
- Roll out on a floured surface to ¾ inch thick. Cut into rounds or squares, dipping the cutter into flour frequently to keep the dough from sticking to it.
- Place on prepared baking sheet.
- Brush with buttermilk.
- Sprinkle tops with brown sugar.
- Bake for 12-14 minutes, or until golden brown.
- To make the glaze, whisk together the bourbon, water, and instant coffee.
- Stir in the powdered sugar, until smooth.
- Drizzle over slightly cooled biscuits.

Sweet and Savory Bread Puddin'

Bread puddin' was a once-a-year treat at my house durin' the Thanksgiving holiday. I couldn't wait for it to be put on the dessert table. Not many folks would think of bread puddin' for breakfast, and that's exactly why I decided to put my twist on it. I've come up with a sweet and savory combination that will have you questionin' ever'thing you thought you knew about breakfast and bread puddin'.

Serves 12

INGREDIENTS:

Nonstick cooking spray
1 lb. breakfast sausage
3 apples, any variety, peeled and cubed
3 jalapenos, seeds removed, diced
1/2 tsp. fresh grated or ground ginger
3 tbsp. butter
3 cups milk or half-and-half
6 eggs, beaten
2 tbsp. maple syrup
6 cups cubed any day-old bread

This can also be made with bacon or ham instead of sausage.

SAUCE:

1/2 cup butter
1 cup maple syrup
Zest of 1/2 orange
1/2 cup powdered sugar, for topping

DIRECTIONS:

- Preheat oven to 375 degrees and spray a 9x13 baking dish with nonstick cooking spray.

- In a Dutch oven or similar pot over medium heat, cook and crumble sausage until done.

- Add the apples, jalapenos, and ginger; stir and cook for 5 minutes.

- Turn off heat and add the butter, stirring until melted. Pour in the milk, eggs, and syrup; stir to combine.

- Add the bread and toss until well combined. Transfer to prepared dish.

- Bake for 30-35 minutes or until it is medium brown and still jiggles slightly.

- Place the sauce ingredients in a saucepan and cook over low heat until butter is melted.

- Remove bread pudding from oven and pour sauce over. Spoon servings onto plates, and dust with powdered sugar.

Sweet Tater Fritters

My Grandpa and Grandma Creech had sweet taters at just about ever' meal. They even fried 'em up for breakfast. Whenever they had leftover sweet taters, Grandma Creech would make sweet tater cakes, by just addin' flour and egg and tossin' 'em in a fryin' pan. To give Grandma's tater cakes a twist, I thought I would add some spices and fry them up into crispy fritters. I think she'd be proud of these tasty li'l bites that she helped inspire.

Serves 4-6

INGREDIENTS:

2 cups mashed sweet taters
1 egg
1 tsp. vanilla
1/2 cup cornmeal
2 tbsp. all-purpose flour
1 tbsp. brown sugar
1/2 tsp. ground cinnamon
Butter for frying, about 1/2 cup

SAUCE:

1 cup maple syrup
2 tbsp. butter, melted
1/2 tsp. ground cinnamon
Pinch of salt

These can be fried the day before and warmed up the next morning. They also work great for dessert with a scoop of your favorite ice cream.

DIRECTIONS:

- Place the sauce ingredients in a bowl and whisk together.

- In a mixing bowl, stir the taters, egg, and vanilla until combined.

- Stir in the cornmeal, flour, sugar, and cinnamon.

- In a medium skillet over medium heat, melt half the butter.

- Using an ice-cream scoop, place 4 scoops batter in hot butter, making sure they are separated.

- Fry for 3-4 minutes or until edges start to brown. Flip and fry another 3-4 minutes until brown. Transfer to a serving plate. Repeat until all the batter is gone.

- Drizzle sauce over fritters and serve warm.

Tasty Tater Casserole

Taters are usually used in standalone dishes, but they are great for making casseroles hearty and tasty. The twist on this breakfast casserole is that y'all can make it your own by addin' your favorite meats, veggies, cheeses, and spices. It is literally a full-course meal in one pan. Make breakfast easy—just dump tasty ingredients in with a heapin' pile of tater tots, and get ready for a stampede to the breakfast table.

Serves 12

This can be made without meat as well.

INGREDIENTS:

Nonstick cooking spray
1 lb. bacon, coarsely chopped, divided
1 medium yellow onion, diced
1 cup chopped white button mushrooms
1 red bell pepper, diced
1 (32 oz.) bag tater tots
3 cups shredded Monterey Jack cheese, divided
7 eggs, slightly beaten
$\frac{1}{2}$ cup canned evaporated milk
$\frac{1}{2}$ can cream of mushroom soup
$\frac{1}{2}$ tsp. salt
$\frac{1}{2}$ tsp. ground black pepper
$\frac{1}{2}$ tsp. garlic powder
1 tsp. poultry seasoning
$\frac{1}{2}$ cup sliced green onions

DIRECTIONS:

- Preheat oven to 375 degrees and spray a 9x13 baking dish with nonstick cooking spray.

- In a skillet over medium heat, cook chopped bacon until crispy. Remove bacon to a paper-towel-lined plate.

- Add the onions, mushrooms, and peppers to the skillet and sauté for 5-8 minutes, stirring often. You just want the veggies to be tender.

- Lay the tater tots in the baking dish in as much of a single layer as possible.

- Sprinkle half the cheese and half the bacon over the tater tots.

- In a mixing bowl, stir the eggs, milk, cream soup, and seasonings, and sautéed veggies until combined. Pour over tots.

- Bake for 35-40 minutes or until eggs are set. Remove from oven and sprinkle the rest of the cheese and bacon over the top. Bake another 5-6 minutes, just until the cheese is melted.

- Remove from oven, let stand for 10 minutes, then garnish with green onions.

Chapter 2
MIXED FILLIN'S
(SALADS AND SANDWICHES)

Caprese 'Mater Panini

Connie's Jeweled Cranberry Salad

Country Ham and Beer-Cheese Sammy

Deviled Egg-Salad Sandwich

Easy Pea'sy Salad

Festive Warm Pasta Salad

Fried Green 'Mater and Bacon Samich

Grilled BBQ Baloney Sandwich

Hobo Salad Sandwich

'Mater-Melon Salad

Maxine's Summer Tuna Salad

Mom's Slaw

Not Momma's Tater Salad

New Country Cornbread Salad

Roasted Beets and Goat Cheese Salad

Pimento-Cheese Waffle Sandwich

Southern-Soul Ham Salad

Spiced Sweet Tater Salad

Sweet and Tangy Broccoli Salad

Uptown Black-Eyed Pea Salad

Warm Kale and Butternut Squash Salad

Warm Bacon and Mustard Salad Dressing

Children, let me tell ya somethin' about salads in the South: no lettuce required. We call anything that can be tossed or held together with mayo or gelatin a salad. And Lord knows we'll make anything into a sandwich, even our salads. And before ya go thinkin' that the difference between a sandwich and a salad is the bread, *don't get too big for your britches,* 'cause we even put bread in our salads. So y'all can see that the line between salads and sandwiches in the South can get mighty blurred sometimes.

Now don't worry your pretty little heads tryin' to figure it all out—I've gotcha covered. Whether you're plannin' a lovely ladies' brunch, lunch for the fam, a potluck dinner, or an awesome tailgating spread, my special *twists* on traditional Southern sammies and salads will be just the ticket.

Caprese 'Mater Panini

Growin' up, I loved a cheese sandwich with a fresh garden 'mater. Who knew this was the beginning of my love for caprese salads, which happen to be my inspiration for this twist: an upscale grilled cheese sandwich with all the flavors of a caprese salad.

Serves 4

INGREDIENTS:
1 cup mayo
8 slices sourdough bread
8 slices fresh mozzarella cheese
8 slices fresh heirloom tomatoes
16 fresh basil leaves
3 cups arugula lettuce
$\frac{1}{2}$ cup butter, softened

BALSAMIC GLAZE:
1 cup balsamic vinegar
1 tbsp. light brown sugar

If you don't have a panini press, you can heat two cast-iron skillets, place the sandwich in one and put the second skillet on top, and mash down.

DIRECTIONS:
- Place the balsamic glaze ingredients in a saucepan over medium heat. Reduce by half, stirring often. Do not boil. When reduced, take off heat and let cool.

- Once cooled, mix 2 tbsp. balsamic glaze with the mayo. Reserve remaining glaze.

- Place 4 slices bread on parchment paper, and spread a thin layer of the mayo over bread. Place 2 slices cheese, 2 slices tomatoes, and 4 basil leaves on each bread slice. Add small amount of arugula on top of each. Spread another thin layer of mayo on the other 4 slices bread and put on top of sandwich.

- Preheat a panini press. When press is hot, brush with butter. Place 1 sandwich on the press and brush the top of bread with butter. Close lid and press down. Cook for 2-3 minutes. Remove the sandwich, cut in half, and place on a serving platter.

- Repeat until all sandwiches are cooked. Then drizzle reserved balsamic glaze over tops or serve on the side.

Connie's Jeweled Cranberry Salad

During the Thanksgivin' and Christmas holidays, my mom, Connie, would always make this festive-lookin' salad. I've added pineapple to give a tropical twist to one of my mom's signature recipes.

Serves 8

INGREDIENTS:
1 large box raspberry gelatin
2 cups boiling water
1 (14 oz.) can whole cranberry sauce
1 (20 oz.) can crushed pineapple, undrained
1 large red or yellow apple, cored and diced
2 ribs celery, chopped
1 cup chopped pecans, divided

Experiment with some of your favorite fruits.

DIRECTIONS:
- Place the gelatin in a large bowl and dissolve with boiling water. Add cranberry sauce; mix until melted.

- Stir in the pineapples, apples, celery, and half of the pecans.

- Pour into a serving dish or mold, and sprinkle top with remaining pecans. Cover and set in fridge until firm. This will take at least 3 hours.

Country Ham and Beer-Cheese Sammy

Growin' up, we raised hogs to kill in the fall, so we'd have meat all winter. My Grandpa and Grandma Creech would prepare country hams and hang 'em in the smokehouse, where they would cure to perfection. Now ever'one loves a good ham and cheese sandwich, but my twist of toppin' a salty slice of country ham with a hoppy, homemade beer cheese is like goin' from paint-by-numbers to a Picasso.

Serves 4-6

INGREDIENTS:

1 bottle pale ale beer, stale
½ white onion, chopped
1 tsp. minced fresh garlic
1 lb. shredded sharp cheddar cheese
1 tbsp. Worcestershire sauce
1 tsp. cayenne pepper
½ tsp. onion salt
1 tsp. dry mustard
6 pretzel buns
12 slices cooked country ham, fried to caramelized brown

Add a slice of tomato and pickled onions to take this up a level.

DIRECTIONS:

- Make sure to let the beer get stale before making this, by leaving it out and open for 1-2 hours.

- In a food processor, pulse the onion and garlic until superfine. Then add the cheese, Worcestershire sauce, cayenne, onion salt, and dry mustard. Pulse until well combined.

- With the food processor running, slowly add the beer. Mix until cheese reaches a smooth, creamy consistency—it usually takes about half the bottle of beer.

- Remove cheese and put into a container with a lid.

- To make the sandwiches, spread enough beer cheese on bottom buns to cover from edge to edge; I like mine about a half-inch thick. Place 2 slices country ham on each bottom bun, spread a little beer cheese on top of the ham, and cover with top bun.

Deviled Egg-Salad Sandwich

No respectable Southern potluck or family dinner would be complete without deviled eggs. Is it just a coincidence that a good deviled egg can also be turned into a great egg-salad sandwich? I think not. I think it's a divine plan to put deviled eggs in their place—between two slices of a flaky croissant. I've given a basic deviled egg recipe a twist, *by addin' a li'l of this and a li'l of that to create a heavenly deviled egg-salad sandwich.*

Serves 6

INGREDIENTS:

¼ cup sweet pickle relish
2 tbsp. dill pickle relish
4 oz. diced pimentos, drained
⅓ cup mayo
2 tsp. wholegrain mustard
½ tsp. salt
½ tsp. ground white pepper
Dash of cayenne pepper (optional)
12 hardboiled eggs, coarsely chopped
½ cup finely diced celery
½ cup chopped green onions
6 large croissants, sliced lengthwise
Paprika, for garnish

This makes a great treat for brunch when served in lettuce cups.

DIRECTIONS:

- In a mixing bowl, stir together both kinds of pickle relish, pimentos, mayo, mustard, salt, and peppers until combined.

- Add the eggs, celery, and onions. Fold to combine.

- Spoon egg salad onto croissants, sprinkle with paprika, and serve.

Easy Pea'sy Salad

Have trouble gettin' ever'body on board with peas? Well, throw some bright green peas in with other colorful vegetables, bacon, cheese, and creamy ranch dressing, and you may convert even the staunchest of pea-haters. My twist with peas is simple: just toss fresh or frozen peas into a tasty salad, and toss storebought canned peas out the door.

Serves 6

INGREDIENTS:

1 cup real bacon bits
1/2 cup chopped purple onion
1/4 cup chopped orange bell pepper
3 cups frozen peas, thawed
1 cup frozen whole-kernel white or yellow corn, thawed
3/4 cup sour cream
1 pkg. dry ranch dressing seasoning
1 cup finely shredded Colby-Jack cheese
1/2 cup toasted almonds, rough chopped

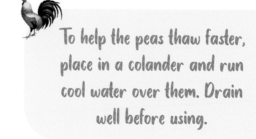

To help the peas thaw faster, place in a colander and run cool water over them. Drain well before using.

DIRECTIONS:

- In a bowl, toss together the bacon, onion, bell pepper, peas, and corn.

- In a small bowl, whisk together sour cream and ranch seasoning.

- Add the cheese to the vegetables, and stir in the dressing.

- Transfer to a serving bowl and sprinkle with almonds.

Festive Warm Pasta Salad

When my granny made tater salad, she made a cooked mustard dressin' to put on it. It was so good that I could eat the entire bowlful at one time. I love pasta salads, so it was only natural for me to borrow her recipe and give it a twist by takin' pasta with veggies and bacon, and givin' it a good toss in Granny's warm mustard dressin'.

Serves 6-8

INGREDIENTS:

2 cups uncooked bowtie pasta
2 cups diced bacon
1 small to medium purple onion, minced
1 tbsp. brown mustard
2 tbsp. honey
¼ cup apple cider vinegar
1 green bell pepper, diced
Good pinch of crushed red pepper flakes (optional)
½ cup dried cranberries
1 cup pecans, chopped

You can add diced grilled chicken to this for a one-dish meal.

DIRECTIONS:

- Cook pasta according to package instructions. Drain and place in a mixing bowl.

- In a large skillet over medium heat, cook bacon until crispy. Remove bacon and set aside.

- Add the onion to the pan, and cook for 4-5 minutes.

- Add the mustard, honey, and vinegar, and stir to combine.

- Pour the pasta into the skillet and toss to coat.

- Remove from heat and stir in bell pepper, red pepper flakes, and cranberries.

- Spoon into a serving bowl, and top with the pecans and cooked bacon.

Fried Green 'Mater and Bacon Samich

'Maters and bacon are truly a match made in heaven—hello, BLT. Fried green 'maters are a bona-fide Southern delicacy, and I think we all know how I feel about bacon. So, is there any wonder that I decided to do a twist by pairin' Southern-fried green 'maters with crisp, smoky bacon and givin' it a li'l zing with some lemon aioli? I promise y'all, it's one of my all-time favorites. After y'all taste it, you'll be growin' 'maters just to pick 'em before they ever get ripe.

Serves 4-6

INGREDIENTS:

3 medium green tomatoes, washed and sliced 1 inch thick
1 tbsp. salt
2 tsp. ground black pepper
1 tsp. paprika
¼ tsp. garlic powder
1 lb. sliced bacon
½ cup brown sugar
½ tsp. cayenne pepper
Oil for frying
1 cup white or yellow cornmeal
1 cup white or yellow grits
1 pkg. wholegrain buns
½ head romaine lettuce, shredded

When cooking bacon, baking in the oven is the least messy method and makes it crispy.

AIOLI:

1 cup mayo
Zest of ½ lemon
1 tsp. smoked paprika

DIRECTIONS:

- On a paper-towel-lined baking sheet, lay tomato slices flat.

- Mix together the salt, pepper, paprika, and garlic powder. Sprinkle half the mixture over the tomato slices, flip, and repeat on the other side.

- Let stand for 15-20 minutes.

- Preheat oven to 350 degrees. On a foil-lined baking sheet, lay the bacon in a single layer. Sprinkle the brown sugar and cayenne evenly over the bacon and bake for 20-25 minutes.

- Pour about 1 inch oil into a cast-iron skillet, and heat over medium heat.

- In a shallow dish, make a dry breading by stirring the cornmeal and grits until combined.

- Press tomato slices into the dry breading. Repeat on the other side.

- Place 5-6 slices tomatoes into the oil, and fry for 4-5 minutes per side or until golden brown.

- Remove to a paper-towel-lined baking sheet. Repeat until all tomatoes are fried.

- Place the aioli ingredients in a small mixing bowl and whisk.

- Lay 4 to 6 bun bottoms on a platter.

- Place 2 slices fried tomatoes on each, followed by 2-3 strips bacon, then a small amount of lettuce.

- Spread the bun tops with aioli and place on each tomato-bacon stack.

Grilled BBQ Baloney Sandwich

It may be B-O-L-O-G-N-A to some of y'all, but to me, it's just good ol' baloney. Lordy, I remember eatin' fried baloney for breakfast and fried baloney sandwiches for lunch. I swear I'd have eaten it three times a day if my momma would have let me. I decided to give this old-fashioned favorite a twist by grillin' it with a homemade BBQ sauce and addin' a salty crunch by toppin' it with tater chips.

Serves 4

INGREDIENTS:

1 cup ketchup
¼ cup prepared yellow mustard
2 tbsp. honey
2 tsp. chili powder
1 tsp. onion powder
3 tbsp. butter, melted
2 tbsp. steak sauce
4 (1 inch) thick slices old-fashioned bologna
4 cornmeal-dusted buns
4 slices yellow American cheese
1 ripe tomato, sliced
Leaves of butter lettuce
1 bag plain potato chips
½ cup mayo

You can use any flavor chips you like.

DIRECTIONS:

- Preheat grill to medium.

- In a mason jar, place the ketchup, mustard, honey, chili powder, onion powder, butter, and steak sauce. Put on lid and shake to combine.

- Place the bologna on grill and spread with the BBQ sauce. Flip and spread more BBQ sauce on other side, reserving some sauce. Grill bologna until bubbly and brown.

- Place 1 bologna slice on 1 bun bottom. Top with 1 slice cheese. Top with the tomato, lettuce, and a handful of chips. Drizzle a little BBQ sauce over chips. Spread 1 bun top with some of the mayo and place on the sandwich. Repeat with remaining ingredients.

Hobo Salad Sandwich

Hobo salad is traditionally made with baloney or ham. It was considered a cheap way to stretch a meal, and that is probably how it gained its name. Some folks may call it "poor man's salad." No matter what you call it, it has earned its place in Southern culture and deserves to be recognized as an honest-to-good sandwich. This is a traditional recipe, but y'all can give it a twist by adding whatever deli meat and ingredients you have on hand.

Serves 6-8

INGREDIENTS:
2 lb. bologna or ham
6-8 whole dill pickles
1/4 cup minced yellow or white onion
1/2-3/4 cup real mayo
1/2 tsp. ground black pepper
Slices of white potato bread

Add your favorite
sandwich toppings.

DIRECTIONS:
- In a food processor, pulse the bologna and pickles until coarsely chopped.

- Transfer to a mixing bowl and stir in the onion, mayo, and pepper.

- Toast the bread in a toaster or under a broiler.

- Spread some of the hobo salad on 1 slice bread and top with a second slice. Repeat with remaining salad and bread.

'Mater-Melon Salad

The summer garden brings two of my favorite things: 'maters and watermelon. I could sit and eat my weight in both. A lot of folks are skeptical when I tell 'em that I like to eat 'maters with my melon, but trust me, it's a match made in fruit heaven. After all, in case y'all didn't know, a 'mater is a fruit. I always like a big bowl of quartered 'maters and cubed watermelon with fresh basil as one of my summer snacks. When I got to thinkin' about it, I realized that this snack could be twisted into a scrumptious salad. It won't take long for y'all to get on my 'mater-melon bandwagon, after you wrap your tongue around this fresh summertime treat.

Serves 4-6

Try to use heirloom tomatoes, as they give lots of color and flavor.

INGREDIENTS:

4 cups watermelon balls or cubes
½ cup diced purple onion
2 orange or yellow tomatoes, diced
1 pint mixed-color cherry tomatoes, halved lengthwise
8-10 leaves fresh basil, chopped
2 tbsp. canola oil
3 tbsp. balsamic vinegar
2 tbsp. honey
Salt and ground black pepper to taste
2 cups crumbled feta cheese

DIRECTIONS:

- In a large bowl, combine the watermelon, onion, tomatoes, and basil.

- Whisk together the oil, vinegar, honey, salt, and pepper.

- Pour over salad and toss to coat.

- Sprinkle with cheese and serve, or place in the fridge until ready to serve.

Maxine's Summer Tuna Salad

Sometimes, on a hot summer day, a light lunch is just the ticket. My friend Mark introduced me to this recipe. His mother, Maxine, had made it for him since he was a kid. Now, I'm not gonna lie—I couldn't imagine peas in my tuna salad, that is until I tasted this light and refreshin' twist that Maxine had created. I think of Maxine ever'time I make this, and I know that Mark does too. Ain't it so comfortin' how food memories bring back those we love?

Serves 4

INGREDIENTS:

1 head iceberg lettuce, chopped
2 cans tuna in water, drained
1 medium onion, diced
2 cups frozen peas, thawed
¾ cup mayo
Salt and ground black pepper to taste

This can also be made
with chicken.

DIRECTIONS:

- In a large mixing bowl, toss all ingredients together.
- Place in a container with a lid and let stand in fridge for several hours or overnight.
- Serve with crackers.

Mom's Slaw

In the South, when you think of slaw, you usually think of cabbage laden with creamy mayo; and by laden, I mean get the shovel out. My mom put her twist on traditional coleslaw with the light and tangy dressing in this recipe. Some folks call this type of recipe vinegar-slaw, but since I've eaten my momma's version, I just call it "Mom's Slaw."

Serves 8-12

INGREDIENTS:

1 medium head green cabbage
1 red bell pepper, chopped
1 medium purple onion, diced
¾ cup white sugar
½ cup canola oil
¼ cup white or apple cider vinegar
1 tsp. salt
1 tsp. ground black pepper

The longer this slaw sets,
the better it gets.

DIRECTIONS:

- Shred cabbage and transfer to a mixing bowl. Place the bell pepper and onion on top of the cabbage.
- In a small mixing bowl, whisk the sugar, oil, vinegar, salt, and pepper.
- Pour over cabbage mixture, and stir to combine. Place in an airtight container and set in fridge for several hours or overnight.

Not Momma's Tater Salad

If there's one salad that ever'one claims to have the best recipe for, it's tater salad. I mean, who knows, it may be the real cause of some pretty famous family feuds in my home state of Kentucky. The debate over the best traditional tater salad may be eternal, but children, I can tell y'all who makes the best nontraditional tater salad that I've ever put in my pie-hole: my good friend Wayne from Louisville, Kentucky. He's really put his twist on your momma's tater salad, or as my mom would say, that Wayne has really put his toe in this one.

Serves 8-10

INGREDIENTS:
3 lb. red-skinned potatoes
Salt
1 lb. bacon, cooked and chopped
1 cup green salad olives, sliced in half
1 (8 oz.) block marble cheddar cheese, cubed small
1 orange bell pepper, diced
2 tbsp. celery seed
1 cup mayo

GARNISH:
Green salad olives
Cooked and chopped bacon

If doing low carb, you can use 2 heads cauliflower, cut into small florets and blanched, in place of potatoes.

DIRECTIONS:
- Wash potatoes and place in a large pot. Add a touch of salt, cover with water, and cook until tender. Drain and let cool, then cut into small cubes. *Do not peel.*

- In a large mixing bowl, toss the potatoes, bacon, olives, cheese, pepper, and celery seed to combine.

- Add mayo, and mix until all ingredients are well coated. (It may take a little more mayo.)

- Transfer to a serving dish. Cover and set in fridge for at least 4 hours or overnight.

- Garnish with more olives and cooked bacon.

New Country Cornbread Salad

Remember, I told y'all in the intro to this chapter that we ain't afraid to throw bread in and call it a salad, and I ain't talkin' about croutons. I'm talkin' about a big ol' pone of homemade cornbread as the star of this Country Bling twist on salad. Now, the concept of cornbread salad ain't nothin' new to us. As a matter of fact, it's pretty dang popular at potlucks and family dinners. It might sound kinda wacky, but I promise that once y'all taste it, you'll see cornbread and salad in a whole new light.

Serves 6

INGREDIENTS:
8-10 cups cubed cornbread
6-8 strips bacon, diced and cooked, divided
2 tbsp. bacon drippings
½ purple onion, minced
1 cup diced tomatoes
1 bell pepper, any color, diced
1 can black-eyed peas, black beans, or pintos, drained
2 cups shredded cheddar cheese
1 cup mayo
1 cup sour cream
1 tsp. ground black pepper
½ jalapeno, minced (optional)
2 cups cubed deli ham

You can also use ranch dressing in place of the mayo and sour cream.

DIRECTIONS:

- In a large mixing bowl, toss the cornbread with half the bacon and all the bacon drippings.

- Add the onion, tomatoes, bell pepper, peas, and cheese over cornbread. Toss to combine.

- Add the mayo, sour cream, pepper, jalapeno, and ham. Toss until all the cornbread is coated and ingredients are well mixed.

- Pour into a serving bowl. Sprinkle the rest of the bacon over the top.

Roasted Beets and Goat Cheese Salad

My first memories of beets were of the pickled variety. As I've gotten older, I've come to appreciate just how versatile beets are. I love roasted beets by themselves or added to a salad. My twist on beets is to give 'em the starring role in their very own sweet and tangy salad. The simple pairin' of roasted beets and fresh, creamy goat cheese may be the best thing since peanut butter met jelly.

Serves 6-8

INGREDIENTS:
Nonstick cooking spray
5 medium to large fresh beets
2 tbsp. olive oil
2 tsp. dried thyme, or 1 tbsp. fresh thyme, minced
1 tsp. ground black pepper
$\frac{1}{2}$ cup honey or agave
$\frac{1}{4}$ cup butter or coconut oil
3 tbsp. balsamic vinegar
6 oz. goat cheese, crumbled

GARNISH:
Balsamic vinegar
$\frac{1}{2}$ cup pecans or walnuts

When working with beets, always make sure to cut or peel them under running water. This will keep your hands from turning a beautiful shade of ruby red.

DIRECTIONS:
- Preheat oven to 350 degrees. Line a baking sheet with foil and spray with nonstick cooking spray. Also spray a 9x13 baking dish.
- Cut the top off the beets, leaving about 1 inch of the top.
- Place on foil-lined pan and drizzle oil over them. Bring the sides of the foil up to form a package, and seal.
- Roast for 30-40 minutes or until tender.
- When tender, remove from oven and, under cold running water, peel the skin off the beets (it will slip right off).
- Slice beets into half-inch slices, and place in prepared baking dish.
- Sprinkle beets with thyme and pepper.
- Drizzle the honey over the beets.
- Dot the butter around on the top.
- Bake for 30 minutes.
- Remove and drizzle the balsamic vinegar over the top, stirring lightly to coat all pieces.
- Return to oven and bake for 20 minutes.
- Transfer to a serving platter and sprinkle the goat cheese over the top.
- Drizzle with more balsamic vinegar.
- Sprinkle on pecans or walnuts.

Pimento-Cheese Waffle Sandwich

In the county where I grew up, they gave out food items once a month, called commodities, to help folks out. Let me tell y'all, you ain't had 'mentor cheese, as I call it, any better than when it was made with that government commodity cheese. Some of y'all know what I'm talkin' about. I loved 'mentor cheese with crackers or on a white-bread sandwich. To give this traditional Southern spread a twist, I decided to make it a bit creamier and present it on a crunchy, cornmeal waffle. Let me tell y'all, these li'l sammies are the bomb-diggity-bombs *of 'mentor-cheese sandwiches.*

Serves 4-6

INGREDIENTS:
4 cups shredded cheddar cheese
1 cup shredded Colby-Jack cheese
¼ cup mayo
4 oz. cream cheese, room temp
½ tsp. onion powder
½ tsp. garlic powder
Salt and ground black pepper to taste
6 oz. pimentos, diced

This pimento cheese keeps great in the fridge to enjoy for several days.

WAFFLES:
1 cup self-rising white or yellow cornmeal
⅓ cup milk
⅔ cup water or chicken broth
2 tbsp. butter, melted
Nonstick cooking spray

SANDWICH SPREAD:
2 tbsp. butter, melted
¼ cup mayo

DIRECTIONS:
- In a medium mixing bowl, stir cheeses, mayo, and cream cheese to combine.
- Add onion powder, garlic powder, salt, and pepper and stir.
- Stir in the pimentos.
- Place in an airtight container and set aside while making waffle batter.
- Preheat a waffle iron.
- In a small mixing bowl, whisk together the cornmeal, milk, and water.
- Stir in the butter.
- Spray waffle iron with nonstick cooking spray, and place 2-3 tbsp. batter in each well.
- Cook until very golden brown. Repeat until all batter is gone.
- Mix together the sandwich spread ingredients.
- Brush half of mixture on one side of the cooked waffles and set aside.
- Heat skillet or griddle to medium heat.
- Place the mayo-mixture side of waffle down in skillet, and top with 3-4 tbsp.

pimento-cheese mix. Spread some mayo mixture onto the top waffle and place over pimento cheese, with mayo mixture facing up.

- Grill on both sides until medium brown and cheese is melted.

- Repeat with remaining waffles.

Southern-Soul Ham Salad

I'm sure y'all have learned by now that the South does not live on tuna and chicken salad alone. Any meat is fair game to be tossed in mayo and pickle relish and be called a salad. Being the centerpiece of many Southern dinners, with leftovers, ham is one of those meats. I mean, doesn't ever'one take leftover meat and turn it into a salad that can be eaten as a sandwich? Remember, I told y'all the lines can be blurred when it comes to salads and sandwiches.

Serves 6-8

INGREDIENTS:
1 cup real mayo
1/3 cup sweet pickle relish
2 tbsp. Dijon mustard
1/4 cup minced celery
1/4 cup minced yellow or white onion
1 tbsp. light brown sugar
1 tsp. onion powder
1 tsp. garlic salt
2 tbsp. fresh dill, minced
2 hardboiled eggs, chopped
6 cups shredded ham
Sliced country white bread or wheat bread

If you don't have shredded deli ham, place whole ham pieces into a food processor and pulse until desired texture.

DIRECTIONS:
- In a mixing bowl, stir the mayo, pickle relish, mustard, celery, onions, brown sugar, onion powder, garlic salt, dill, and eggs to mix.
- Fold in the ham. Spread on bread or crackers.

Spiced Sweet Tater Salad

Sweet taters ain't just for the traditional sweet tater pie and casserole anymore. Anything y'all can do with a white tater can be done with a sweet tater: mashed, fried, baked, roasted, and with my twist, turned into tater salad. This sweet tater salad is full of fruit, veggies, and spices that add up to a refreshin' and surprisin' slap in the taste buds.

Serves 6

INGREDIENTS:
3 large sweet taters, peeled and cubed
4 tbsp. butter
½ cup chopped green onions
1 red apple, diced
1 yellow bell pepper, diced

LEMON DRESSING:
⅔ cup olive oil
Juice of 1 lemon
1 tsp. lemon zest
1 tbsp. honey
1 tsp. salt
½ tsp. ground white pepper
1 tbsp. minced fresh thyme
½ tsp. garlic powder

GARNISH:
1 cup toasted sunflower seeds

Adding some grilled chicken on the side makes this a great power lunch.

DIRECTIONS:
- In a microwave-proof bowl, place the cubed sweet taters and add butter. Cover and microwave until fork tender. Remove and let cool to room temp.
- In a large mixing bowl, combine green onions, apple, bell pepper, and cooled sweet taters.
- Whisk together the dressing ingredients. Drizzle over veggies and toss to coat. Transfer to a serving bowl and sprinkle the sunflower seeds over the top.

Sweet and Tangy Broccoli Salad

Most folks have always thought that the only way to enjoy broccoli is to cover it with cheese or drown it in ranch dressin'. I'm happy to say that broccoli is finally gettin' its just desserts, by bein' showcased as the main ingredient in some very tasty salads. My twist on broccoli salad is to skip the standard creamy dressin' in favor of a sweet and tangy poppy-seed vinaigrette. This salad will have your head spinnin' with all its textures and flavors, so don't blame me if your hair gets messed up.

Serves 6-8

INGREDIENTS:
2 large heads fresh broccoli
½ cup Craisins
½ cup slivered almonds
½ cup thinly sliced celery
1 tbsp. celery seed
½ cup poppy-seed dressing
½ cup red wine vinaigrette salad dressing

If you have time, soak the broccoli in ice water for a couple of hours, then drain. This allows the broccoli to get real crisp.

DIRECTIONS:
- Cut broccoli into small florets.
- In a large mixing bowl, combine all the ingredients and toss to coat with dressing.
- You may need a touch more dressing for more absorption.
- Transfer to a serving bowl. Cover and set in fridge for at least 2 hours.

Uptown Black-Eyed Pea Salad

Lord Honey, don't y'all dare think of startin' the new year without the epitome of Southern soul food, black-eyed peas. Every Southerner worth his salt knows that eatin' black-eyed peas on New Year's Day ushers in good luck for the year. My aunt Brenda made a salad with black-eyed peas in it, and I've used it as my inspiration in this tasty twist on the South's good-luck legume.

Serves 8

INGREDIENTS:
2 cans (15.5 oz.) black-eyed peas, drained
1 can diced tomatoes, drained
1 cup finely chopped cabbage
2 ribs celery, diced small
½ bunch green onions, sliced
1 cucumber, peeled and diced
1 orange or yellow bell pepper, diced
½ cup grated parmesan cheese

You can add your favorite vegetables to the mix.

DRESSING:
¼ cup vinegar
2-3 tbsp. brown sugar or honey
1 tsp. salt
1 tsp. ground black pepper
1 tsp. onion powder
1 tsp. garlic powder
2 tsp. dried basil
¼ tsp. cayenne pepper (optional)
1 tbsp. Dijon or prepared yellow mustard
2 tbsp. your favorite oil (I use olive oil)

GARNISH:
¼ cup grated parmesan cheese

DIRECTIONS:
- In a mixing bowl, toss the salad ingredients together.
- In a mason jar, place the dressing ingredients. Put on lid and shake several times to combine. Pour over vegetable mix, and toss to coat.
- Transfer to a serving dish. Cover and set in fridge for at least 4 hours.
- When ready to serve, toss and sprinkle parmesan over the top.

Warm Kale and Butternut Squash Salad

Now, I know that the word warm is not what y'all think of when you think of salads, but this salad is my twisted way of enjoyin' one of my favorite fall-harvest foods, butternut squash. We grew all kinds of squash on the farm, storin' them through the winter to make ever'thing from pies to breads, side dishes, and main courses. Once y'all taste the comfortin', fall flavors of this warm salad, you'll be slobberin' like a dog with a bone.

Serves 10

INGREDIENTS:

¼ cup olive oil

3 tbsp. butter

2 medium butternut squash, peeled and cubed small

2 tsp. rubbed sage

1 tsp. ground rosemary

2 tsp. salt

1 tsp. ground black pepper

½ tsp. crushed red pepper flakes

10 cups fresh kale, chopped and large stems removed

8 strips bacon, cubed

Acorn squash or pumpkin can be substituted for the butternut squash.

BACON DRESSING:

Drippings from bacon

2 tbsp. brown mustard

2-3 tbsp. apple cider vinegar

2 tbsp. honey

2 tbsp. bourbon

Salt and ground black pepper to taste

GARNISH:

1½ cups dried cranberries

¼ cup minced purple onion

DIRECTIONS:

- Preheat a large skillet to medium high. Add the oil and butter.

- When butter has melted, add the butternut squash and cook until fork tender, about 20-25 minutes.

- Add the spices and keep cooking squash until totally tender.

- In a large serving bowl, place the chopped kale.

- Spoon the butternut squash over the kale.

- In the same skillet, over medium heat, cook the bacon until crispy. Sprinkle over the vegetables, reserving the bacon drippings in the skillet.

- Whisk the bacon dressing ingredients in the skillet until combined. Cook until the alcohol smell has burned off.

- Drizzle over kale and toss.

- Top with dried cranberries and onions. Serve warm.

Warm Bacon and Mustard Salad Dressing

If I could change the salad world with one thing, it would be to tell ever'one that there is more than one choice when it comes to dressin' your salads. Although that creamy, white concoction that has taken over the condiment world has its place, it is not the end-all, be-all. Your dressin' flavor should pair with the type of salad your havin', not overwhelm it. This twist on my Granny Jean's sweet mustard dressin' gives y'all a dressin' that can be used on almost any salad you're havin', as well as a great sauce for roasted veggies.

Makes 1 cup

INGREDIENTS:

4 strips bacon, minced
3 cloves garlic, minced
3 tbsp. honey or molasses
3 tbsp. wholegrain mustard
¼ cup apple cider vinegar
Pinch of crushed red pepper flakes
1 tsp. coarse-ground black pepper
½ tsp. salt

This dressing is good on vegetables, especially asparagus and Brussels sprouts.

DIRECTIONS:

- In a medium saucepan over low heat, stir the bacon until some of the fat begins to render out. Raise the heat to medium and cook the bacon, stirring frequently, until crispy. Use a slotted spoon to transfer the crisp bacon to a paper-towel-lined plate. Keep all of the fat drippings in the pan.

- Return the pan to the burner. Add the garlic, swirl, and immediately add the remaining ingredients. Bring the mixture to a boil and let it cook for 1 minute, or until the dressing coats the back of a spoon and your finger leaves a trail when you draw it through the dressing on the spoon. Stir in the bacon.

- Use immediately, or transfer to a heat-proof jar with a tight-fitting lid and store in the fridge for up to 5 days. Gently reheat and stir before serving.

Chapter 3

WHAT ELSE?
(SIDES)

'Lasses-Glazed Carrots

Black-Eyed-Pea Patties

Blistered Beans with Bacon and Bourbon

Country Sautéed Onions

Creamy Corn with Bacon

Crispy Smooshed Herbed Taters

Devilish Eggs — Three Ways

Easy Collard Greens

Heirloom-'Mater Galette

New-South Squash Casserole

Pleasin' Pineapple Bake

Southern Five-Bean Bake

Roasted Okra and Walnuts

Southern-Best Hominy

Spicy Corn Puddin'

Southern-Fried Taters and Onions

Stuffin' Muffins

Sunday-Supper Green Beans and 'Maters

Super-Creamy Mac and Cheese Bake

Tasty Fried Turnips

Twice-Baked Sweet Taters

When I would ask Mom what was for dinner, she would usually just answer with roast, or fried chicken, or meatloaf. She always knew what I was gonna ask next: "What else?" For me the "What else?" was as important as the main dish. The "What else?" could make my mouth water in anticipation or snarl in dread. I'm sure y'all have guessed that "What else?" means all the fixin's that go with the meal—what we call the side dishes.

A good side dish, even though it's *playin' second fiddle* to the star, is what brings the elements of your meal together. It's a layerin' of textures, colors, and flavors that balances with the main course to bring home an award-winning meal. Remember, *you can put a pig in a tutu but it doesn't make it a ballerina;* it only makes it pretty. If it don't go together, it just ain't gonna work.

I hope you have fun plannin' your meals with my *twists* on traditional Southern sides.

'Lasses-Glazed Carrots

Granny would always say, "Bring me the 'lasses," when she wanted her jug of molasses from the pantry. Molasses has been used as a sweet'ner in the South for generations. Its sweet taste and syrupy thickness make it a great choice for glazes and sauces.

Serves 4

INGREDIENTS:
1 lb. carrots, washed and ends cut off
3 tbsp. molasses
3 tbsp. balsamic vinegar
3 tbsp. butter, melted
½ tsp. ground black pepper
2 tsp. dried thyme
½ tsp. salt
¼ tsp. crushed red pepper flakes
Zest of ½ lemon

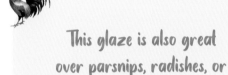

This glaze is also great over parsnips, radishes, or sweet taters.

DIRECTIONS:
- Preheat oven to 400 degrees. Grease a baking sheet with butter.
- Cut the carrots into short, fat sticks and place in a mixing bowl.
- In a small mixing bowl, stir the molasses, vinegar, and butter to combine.
- Pour half the molasses mixture over carrots and toss to coat.
- Sprinkle the pepper, thyme, salt, red pepper flakes, and lemon zest over the carrots and toss.
- Place the carrots on the prepared baking sheet in a single layer.
- Roast in oven for 25 minutes. Remove, drizzle with remaining molasses mixture, and toss to coat. Spread back into a single layer and bake another 25 minutes before serving.

Black-Eyed-Pea Patties

Black-eyed peas are said to bring good luck for the new year. Growin' up, I was only used to eatin' 'em cooked like pinto beans. Now, I loved Mom's cookin', but this just wasn't one of my favorite dishes. That's why I decided to put a twist on the traditional. You can serve my Black-Eyed-Pea Patties as the protein of your meal or as a side that would go well with most meat dishes.

Makes approximately 12 patties

INGREDIENTS:

1 can (15.5 oz.) black-eyed peas, drained
2 eggs
1 small onion, minced
1 tsp. onion powder
½ tsp. ground black pepper
½ tsp. salt
¼ cup self-rising flour
¼ cup self-rising cornmeal
1 jalapeno, minced (seeds optional)
Veggie oil for frying, about 1 cup

These can also be made with pinto beans, black beans, or great Northerns.

DIRECTIONS:

- In a bowl, mash drained peas.

- Mix in the eggs, onion, onion powder, pepper, and salt.

- Stir in the flour, meal, and jalapeno.

- Heat a large skillet over medium heat. I prefer cast iron.

- Add the oil and bring to 350 degrees as indicated on a deep-fry thermometer.

- Scoop 3 balls of mixture using a 3-oz. scoop. Flatten slightly into patties and fry for 4 minutes per side or until medium brown. Drain on a paper-towel-lined plate. Continue frying process until all mixture has been used.

Blistered Beans with Bacon and Bourbon

This twisted *take on a traditional side of green beans was born out of necessity. I was visitin' with friends at the Memphis in May barbecue championship and was asked to prepare a dish to go along with the wonderful hog that the Beached Pig BBQ team had roasted. Seein' what limited ingredients I had to work with, I concocted my Blistered Beans with Bacon and Bourbon. It was a hit with the crowd, and I have been makin' it ever' since.*

Serves 4

INGREDIENTS:

6 strips bacon, cubed
1 lb. fresh green beans, washed and patted dry
2 oz. bourbon
1½ tbsp. balsamic vinegar
1 tbsp. honey
1 tsp. salt
1 tsp. ground black pepper
Pinch of crushed red pepper flakes

This can also be done with asparagus.

DIRECTIONS:

- In a heavy-bottomed or cast-iron skillet over medium heat, cook the bacon until crispy and remove.

- Turn heat to high and add the green beans to the skillet.

- Cook until brown blisters form on skin of beans, tossing often to prevent burning; this takes about 10 minutes. Cooking surfaces may vary, so you may need to adjust temperature setting.

- Add the bourbon, vinegar, and honey, and toss until beans are coated.

- Cook for 2-3 minutes to thicken sauce.

- Sprinkle with salt, pepper, and red pepper flakes.

- Transfer beans to a serving dish and top with bacon.

Country Sautéed Onions

I know most folks would never think of a purely onion side dish. But if y'all had the onions we had in the springtime, you'd figure out something to do with 'em too. Granny would just slice 'em, cook 'em up in a frying pan, and put 'em in a serving dish. I've twisted simple sautéed onions by addin' sweet pearls—pearl onions and sweet brown sugar, that is.

Serves 4

INGREDIENTS:

3 tbsp. butter
2 tbsp. bacon drippings
2 bunches large green onions, chopped
2 small bags frozen pearl onions
2 large, sweet onions, sliced
¼ cup veggie stock
¼ tsp. salt
¼ tsp. ground white pepper
2 tbsp. light brown sugar
¼ cup chopped fresh parsley, for garnish

If you don't have bacon drippings, you can always use more butter.

DIRECTIONS:

- In a large skillet over medium heat, melt the butter in the bacon drippings.

- Add the onions, veggie stock, salt, and pepper. Place a lid on skillet and cook for 5 minutes. Reduce heat to low and continue to cook for 8 minutes.

- Remove lid and stir. Add the brown sugar. Cook, uncovered, for 5 minutes, stirring often to keep from sticking.

- When onions are tender, transfer to a serving platter and sprinkle with chopped parsley.

Creamy Corn with Bacon

The cornfields on our farm went as far as the eye could see. Not only did we grow it to freeze and can for the family to enjoy all year long, but we also had to grow field corn for the livestock. I guess y'all could say I had a corny childhood. Um, that may explain a lot. I loved my aunt Jean's buttery, fried corn. I've given this nostalgic side a twist with some fresh herbs and heavy cream. I think Aunt Jean would approve, and I think y'all will love this more than a squirrel loves nuts.

Serves 8-10

INGREDIENTS:

1 tbsp. bacon drippings
$\frac{1}{2}$ cup butter
1 medium onion, diced
2 pkg. frozen whole-kernel corn
2 tsp. white sugar
1 tsp. salt
$\frac{1}{2}$ tsp. ground white pepper
5-6 sprigs fresh thyme, stems removed
$\frac{1}{2}$ cup heavy cream
2 tsp. cornstarch
$\frac{1}{2}$ lb. bacon, chopped and cooked crispy

Adding diced red bell peppers gives a festive appearance to this dish.

DIRECTIONS:

- In a skillet over medium heat, add the bacon drippings, butter, and onions. Cook onions until tender.

- Stir in the corn, sugar, salt, pepper, and thyme. Cook for 20-25 minutes.

- In a small bowl, stir the cream and cornstarch together until well combined. Add to the corn and cook for 5 minutes.

- Transfer to a serving dish and sprinkle with bacon.

Crispy Smooshed Herbed Taters

If y'all ain't figured it out, taters are the starch staple of the South. This recipe is a fun and flavorful way to enjoy crispy, buttery, herby taters that will melt in your mouth. I like mine with a dollop of sour cream, but y'all can go crazy and give your own twists to how you top this spectacular spud.

Serves 6

INGREDIENTS:

2 lb. small red or golden potatoes
1 cup butter, melted
¼ cup fresh rosemary, minced
2 tbsp. fresh oregano, minced
2 cloves garlic, minced
1 tsp. salt
1 tsp. ground black pepper
1 tsp. smoked paprika

GARNISH:

Fresh rosemary
Sour cream (optional)

If you can't find smoked paprika, regular paprika will work fine.

DIRECTIONS:

- Preheat oven to 400 degrees.

- Wash and dry potatoes and place in a bowl.

- In a separate bowl, combine melted butter, rosemary, oregano, garlic, salt, pepper, and paprika.

- Pour half the butter mixture over potatoes, and toss to coat. Place potatoes on a large baking sheet in a single layer. Roast for 20 minutes or until tender.

- Remove from oven. Using the bottom of a soup can that's been washed and dried, flatten each potato just until it pops open.

- Drizzle the rest of the butter mixture over the potatoes.

- Turn oven to broil. Place potatoes on top rack and broil for 3-4 minutes until desired crispness.

- Transfer to a serving platter, and garnish with fresh rosemary.

- When serving, add a dollop of sour cream or your preferred topping.

DEVILISH EGGS — THREE WAYS

Let me tell y'all why I call my deviled eggs devilish. Bein' from a good Southern Baptist family, my granny cringed at the thought of givin' credit for somethin' so good to somethin' so bad. So, I just decided that "ish" might be a better way to describe 'em: not completely deviled, just devil-ish. We rarely had deviled eggs growin' up, except on special occasions like a church potluck or dinner on the ground (an outside church gatherin' to bring fellowship and food together). Granny didn't like to use her eggs for anything except breakfast or bakin', because she considered 'em too valuable of a commodity. There's an endless number of ways to make deviled eggs, from the traditional to whatever flips your skirt. I'm gonna share a traditional deviled-egg recipe with y'all and two more with my Country Bling twist.

The Perfect Boiled Egg

Before makin' deviled eggs, y'all need to know how to make "The Perfect Boiled Egg."

Makes 6 eggs

INGREDIENTS:
6 cups cold water
6 eggs
1 tbsp. salt
¼ cup white vinegar

DIRECTIONS:

- In a large saucepan, place the water, eggs, salt, and vinegar. Bring to a rolling boil—boil for 2 minutes.

- Remove from heat and cover, let stand for 12 minutes.

- Remove eggs and place in an ice-water bath until cool.

Traditional Deviled Eggs

No twist here, just tradition, with a classic deviled-egg recipe.

Serves 6

INGREDIENTS:
6 Perfect Boiled Eggs (see index)

FILLING:
1 tbsp. mayo
1 tbsp. yellow mustard
1 tsp. white sugar
½ tsp. salt
½ tsp. ground black pepper
2 tbsp. sweet pickle relish
Paprika, for garnish

If you don't want pickle relish, leave it out, but add 1 more tbsp. mayo.

DIRECTIONS:
- Peel eggs and slice in half lengthwise. Remove yolks and place in a mixing bowl. Place egg-white halves on a serving tray.

- Mash yolks with a fork until they look like coarse cornmeal.

- Add the mayo, mustard, sugar, salt, and pepper, and mix well.

- Stir in the pickle relish.

- Place mixture into a piping bag and pipe into each egg-white half.

- Sprinkle with paprika.

Nacho Momma's Deviled Eggs

El twist on this deviled egg is addin' a li'l kick of Southwest flavor.

Serves 6

INGREDIENTS:
6 Perfect Boiled Eggs (see index)

FILLING:
$\frac{1}{2}$ cup mild salsa, drained
1 tbsp. sour cream
$\frac{1}{4}$ cup whole-kernel corn
$\frac{1}{2}$ tsp. cumin
$\frac{1}{2}$ tsp. ground black pepper
$\frac{1}{2}$ tsp. onion powder

GARNISH:
Shredded cheddar cheese
Chopped chives
Sliced black olives

You can make this with any salsa you wish, and you can increase the level of heat by adding cayenne pepper to taste.

DIRECTIONS:
- Peel eggs and slice in half lengthwise. Remove yolks and place in a mixing bowl. Place egg-white halves on a serving tray.
- Mash yolks with a fork until they look like coarse cornmeal.
- Add the salsa, sour cream, corn, cumin, pepper, and onion powder; mix until creamy.
- Place mixture into a piping bag and cut the tip off. Pipe into each egg-white half.
- Garnish with cheese, chives, and olives.

Bacon-Ranch Deviled Eggs

Ever'one likes to add bacon and ranch flavors to almost ever'thing these days, even cocktails. Well, I've jumped on the bandwagon and given deviled eggs a bacon-ranch twist.

Serves 6

INGREDIENTS:
6 Perfect Boiled Eggs (see index)

FILLING:
3 tbsp. sour cream
2 tsp. dry ranch seasoning
½ tsp. ground black pepper
½ cup minced green onions
¾ cup cooked minced bacon, divided
1 green onion, sliced, for garnish

You can use mayo or Greek yogurt in place of the sour cream.

DIRECTIONS:
- Peel eggs and slice in half lengthwise. Remove yolks and place in a mixing bowl. Place egg-white halves on a serving tray.
- Mash yolks with a fork until they look like coarse cornmeal.
- Add the sour cream, ranch seasoning, and pepper; mix until creamy.
- Stir in the onions and ½ cup bacon.
- Place mixture into a piping bag and pipe into each egg-white half.
- Garnish with remaining bacon and sliced green onion.

Easy Collard Greens

Call 'em country, call 'em Southern, or call 'em soul food, just don't forget to call me when y'all fix a big batch of greens. Oh, how my mouth would water when I smelled greens cookin' on the stove. My belly would also rumble, because it took all day to cook 'em and I thought I'd starve before I got to dig into a big bowlful of collards. The best twist to give greens is to make 'em quicker and easier to cook. Y'all can thank me later.

Serves 4

INGREDIENTS:
10 strips bacon, chopped
2 tbsp. butter
1 small onion, finely diced
2 cloves garlic, minced
1 lb. bag chopped collard greens
1½ cups chicken broth
½ tsp. crushed red pepper flakes
1 tbsp. light brown sugar
Salt and ground black pepper to taste

This can be done with any type of greens.

DIRECTIONS:
- In a Dutch oven over medium heat, cook chopped bacon in butter until crispy. Remove 2 tbsp. bacon for garnish.

- Add onion and garlic and cook until softened, about 2-3 minutes.

- Add greens and cook until slightly wilted, about 3-4 minutes.

- Add broth, red pepper flakes, brown sugar, salt, and pepper. Cover and cook over a low simmer for 35-40 minutes or until tender.

- Once tender, transfer to a serving dish and garnish with reserved bacon.

Heirloom 'Mater Galette

What on earth is a galette, you may ask. Well, I can help y'all out with that. A galette is a round, flat pastry base, topped with sweet or savory ingredients and the edges of the pastry turned in. I think of it as a rustic pie, baked without a pan. Speakin' of pie, this recipe is my twist on a real Southern treat, 'mater pie. This is a great side for brunch, lunch, or dinner and will have y'all droolin' like a newborn baby.

Serves 4-6

INGREDIENTS:
1 (9 inch) piecrust, store bought
3 medium heirloom tomatoes
¾ cup sour cream
2 tbsp. minced basil
2 tbsp. minced thyme
2 tbsp. minced dill
¼ cup minced purple onion
½ tsp. salt
½ tsp. ground white pepper
1 cup grated parmesan cheese, divided
1 clove garlic, grated

EGG WASH:
1 egg
2 tsp. water

GARNISH:
¼ cup minced herbs, combined

> If you can't find heirloom tomatoes, use tomatoes in different colors.

DIRECTIONS:
- Preheat oven to 400 degrees. Line a baking sheet with parchment paper. Lay out pie crust on the prepared baking sheet.

- Slice tomatoes into ¼-inch slices, and place in a colander. Sprinkle with some salt—this allows the extra moisture to leach out. Let stand for 12 minutes, then move to a paper-towel-lined tray and pat dry.

- In a mixing bowl, stir together the sour cream, herbs, onion, salt, pepper, ¾ cup cheese, and garlic.

- Spread mixture over piecrust, making sure to leave a 2-inch border around edge. Arrange the sliced tomatoes over the sour cream layer.

- Bring the edges of the dough up over the edge of the filling, crimping the edges as desired.

- In a small bowl, use a fork to slightly scramble the egg and water.

- Brush the edges of the dough with the egg wash. Sprinkle with the reserved cheese.

- Place the galette in freezer for 10-12 minutes. This allows the fats in the dough to firm back up.

- Bake for 30-35 minutes or until bubbly and crust is golden brown.

- Remove from oven and let rest for 5 minutes. Then transfer to a serving stand and garnish with herbs.

New-South Squash Casserole

Aunt Jean was the squash queen. She would make all kinds of dishes with this fall favorite: squash pickles, squash patties, fried squash, zucchini and squash bread. She would toss it in soups and sauces, and Lord only knows what else we ate it in. In honor of Aunt Jean, I've given a casserole twist to this versatile gourd. This'll have y'all tappin' your feet so hard, you might just squash a bug or two.

Serves approximately 12

INGREDIENTS:
3 lb. yellow squash
1 cup diced purple onion
1 can cream of celery soup
1 cup mayo
1 egg
2 cups shredded cheddar cheese
1 tsp. onion powder
1 tsp. salt
2 tsp. ground black pepper

You can add cooked cubed chicken, for a one-pan meal.

TOPPING:
3 cups cheddar crackers, crushed
1 stick butter, melted

DIRECTIONS:
- Preheat oven to 350 degrees. Grease a 9x13 baking dish.
- Slice the squash into small medallions; set aside.
- In a mixing bowl, combine the onions, cream soup, mayo, egg, cheese, onion powder, salt, and pepper.
- Add the squash, and toss to coat.
- Pour into prepared dish, spreading into an even layer.
- Sprinkle the crushed crackers evenly over the top. Drizzle with butter.
- Cover with foil, and bake for 30 minutes. Remove foil and finish baking for about 20 minutes, or until tender.

Pleasin' Pineapple Bake

I didn't eat much pineapple growin' up. It was just somethin' we didn't have much access to. One of my first experiences with pineapple was at a church picnic, when I was a teenager. I thought it was the most exotic thing I'd ever tasted. I actually got up the nerve to ask the lady for her recipe. Come to find out it had been handed down to her; love that. I've taken the idea of this handed-down recipe and given it my own twist. Make it your own and pass it on—keep the recipe cycle movin'.

Serves 8

INGREDIENTS:
Nonstick cooking spray
1 (20 oz.) can pineapple tidbits, drained, juice reserved
¼ cup reserved juice
¼ cup all-purpose flour
½ cup white sugar
1½ cups shredded sharp cheddar cheese
½ tsp. onion powder
½ tsp. ground black pepper
½ cup diced red or green bell pepper
½ cup crushed plain cornflakes

You can use any corn cereal you like.

TOPPING:
2½ cups crushed plain cornflakes
½ cup butter, melted

DIRECTIONS:

· Preheat oven to 350 degrees. Lightly spray a shallow 1-quart baking dish with nonstick cooking spray.

· In a bowl, mix reserved juice and flour until smooth. Add drained pineapple, sugar, cheese, onion powder, pepper, and diced peppers, and stir until combined.

· Gently stir in cornflakes, then spoon mixture into baking dish.

· In same bowl, combine the topping ingredients. Spread the topping mixture evenly over the pineapple mixture.

· Bake for 30-35 minutes or until cheese is melted and cornflakes are starting to brown.

· Serve immediately.

Southern Five-Bean Bake

I ain't ever met a bean I didn't like, so why not put 'em all together and let 'em become good friends? This five-bean bake twist is a great way to feed a crowd. Just make sure your guests go home before the gas kicks in.

Serves 10-12

INGREDIENTS:

1 (16 oz.) can garbanzo beans
1 (15.5 oz.) can pinto beans
1 (15.5 oz.) can black beans
1 (15.5 oz.) can great Northern beans
1 (15.5 oz.) can light red kidney beans
1 (10 oz.) can diced tomatoes with green chilies
1½ tsp. onion powder
½ tsp. ground black pepper
½ tsp. garlic powder
¼ cup honey
3 cups ketchup
2 tbsp. steak sauce
1 tbsp. Worcestershire sauce
2 tbsp. bourbon
1 lb. bacon, diced
1 medium onion, diced

For a vegetarian option, simply leave the bacon out.

DIRECTIONS:

- Preheat oven to 350 degrees. Grease a 9x13 baking dish.
- Drain all the beans and place in a bowl.
- Mix in all the ingredients except the bacon and onion.
- Pour mixture into prepared baking dish.
- Sprinkle the bacon and onion over the top.
- Cover and bake for 45 minutes.
- Uncover and bake another 35 minutes.

Roasted Okra and Walnuts

Okra is one of those things you either love or hate. I can tell y'all if you'll give this twist on okra a chance, you'll become a lover and not a hater. I mean, no one wants to be a hater. My roasted okra with the crunch of walnuts, tang of vinegar, and spice of a hot honey sauce will have y'all wearin' "I Heart Okra" T-shirts.

Serves 4

INGREDIENTS:
2 lb. fresh okra
2 tbsp. olive oil
1 tbsp. butter, melted
2 tsp. apple cider vinegar
2 tsp. lemon pepper seasoning
2 cloves garlic, minced
1 cup whole walnuts

Roasting okra is a good way to eliminate the moisture that causes it to be slimy.

HOT HONEY SAUCE:
¼ cup honey
2 tsp. hot sauce
2 tbsp. butter, melted

DIRECTIONS:
- Preheat oven to 450 degrees. Line a baking sheet with parchment paper, and set aside.
- Wash okra and pat dry. Cut in half lengthwise.
- Place okra in a large mixing bowl. Add oil, butter, and vinegar, and toss to coat.
- Add the lemon pepper, garlic, and walnuts; toss to combine.
- Spread onto prepared baking sheet.
- Bake for 7 minutes. Remove from oven, stir, then bake another 8 minutes. Remove from oven, stir, then bake another 5 minutes. Okra should be tender and just starting to brown.
- Transfer to a serving tray.
- Whisk the sauce ingredients together and drizzle over okra.

Southern-Best Hominy

Hominy is one of my dad's favorite sides. But unfortunately, it's another one of those love-hate foods. So just what is hominy? The simple answer is it's corn—corn that is soaked in a lye solution and washed, with the outer hull breaking off and leavin' only a plumped corn kernel. Now that may not help convince y'all to try it, but I promise there's a reason it's a staple in Southern-country food. It's just plain good—that is, when it's fixed right. Hominy is a good food to take on the flavors you put with it. That's why my twist on hominy is to add a lot of flavor and texture and toss it into a casserole dish.

Serves 4-6

INGREDIENTS:

Nonstick cooking spray
3 tbsp. butter
2 cloves garlic, minced
3 tbsp. all-purpose flour
1 tsp. ground black pepper
½ tsp. ground nutmeg
½ tsp. dry mustard
1½ cups canned evaporated milk
2 cups grated Monterey Jack cheese
1 (15.5 oz.) can white hominy, drained
2 (15.5 oz.) cans yellow hominy, drained
3 slices country ham, cubed and cooked
1 jalapeno, seeded and diced
4 oz. diced pimentos, drained

GARNISH:

Sliced green onions
Cilantro leaves

> Corn is a great substitute for the hominy.

DIRECTIONS:

- Preheat oven to 350 degrees. Spray an 11x7 casserole dish or ovenproof skillet with nonstick cooking spray.

- In a medium skillet over medium heat, melt butter. Add garlic and cook for 1 minute.

- Whisk in flour, pepper, nutmeg, and mustard. Continue to cook until flour is light brown, about 5 minutes.

- Add evaporated milk and cheese. Stir to combine. Continue cooking until sauce starts to thicken, stirring often.

- Remove from heat and fold in hominy, ham, jalapeño, and pimentos. Pour into prepared dish.

- Cover and bake for 20-25 minutes. Uncover and bake another 5 minutes.

- Transfer to a serving dish and garnish with green onions and cilantro.

Spicy Corn Puddin'

Growin' up, I don't remember a church potluck that didn't have corn puddin' galore. Honey, it was a badge of honor for whoever's corn puddin' was gone first. A good corn puddin' recipe is a must for anybody wantin' to have a true Southern, comfort-food spread. I've given my corn puddin' a twist with a kick of chiles and cayenne.

Serves 6-8

INGREDIENTS:

4 eggs
3 tbsp. butter, melted and cooled
⅓ cup honey
½ cup heavy cream
3 tbsp. cornstarch
1 (4 oz.) can diced green chiles
4 cups fresh or frozen whole-kernel corn
1 (15.5 oz.) can white cream-style corn
1 tsp. salt
1 tsp. ground black pepper
¼ tsp. cayenne pepper

Add your favorite hot peppers to give this an even bigger kick.

DIRECTIONS:

- Preheat oven to 375 degrees. Butter a 9x13 baking dish.

- In a mixing bowl, combine the eggs, butter, honey, heavy cream, and cornstarch. Whisk ingredients until there are no lumps of cornstarch.

- Add the remaining ingredients, and stir to combine. Pour into prepared baking dish.

- Bake for 35-40 minutes, until set, jiggly in the center, and browned around the edges.

Southern-Fried Taters and Onions

I really do think that a white tater is the most versatile food on the planet. It may not be the most abundant worldwide, but it'll always get my vote for its many uses. I mean, what other food can y'all use to remove a broken lightbulb, make craft stamps, soothe puffy eyes, and make delicious side dishes? I've kept the twist on this tasty tuber simple: a slight crunch from cornmeal and the added sweetness and heat from onion.

Serves 4

INGREDIENTS:
4 large white potatoes, peeled and sliced
3 tbsp. cornmeal
Salt and ground black pepper to taste
¼ cup veggie oil
2 tbsp. bacon drippings
1 medium onion, diced

You can use sweet taters or golden potatoes in this recipe if you choose.

DIRECTIONS:
- Preheat a skillet over medium heat.

- Place the potatoes in a bowl. Sprinkle in the cornmeal, salt, and pepper, and toss to coat.

- Add oil and bacon drippings to skillet. When hot, add the potatoes. Fry, covered, for 12 minutes or until they start to get tender.

- Add the onions and stir. Continue cooking until potatoes are brown and onions are soft.

Stuffin' Muffins

There's always been a debate over whether it's "stuffin'" or "dressin'." Well, I was always told if you're stuffin' it in the bird, then it's stuffin'. If you're bakin' it in a pan, then it's dressin'. No matter which side of the debate you fall on, I think you'll enjoy my twist of stuffin' dressin' into a muffin pan. Lord have mercy, I'm as confused as a rooster huntin' a hen on a turkey farm.

Makes 1 dozen

INGREDIENTS:

1 lb. sage breakfast sausage
2 medium onions, diced
2 cups diced fresh baby portobella mushrooms
1/2 cup butter
8 cups crumbled cornbread
Salt and ground black pepper to taste
1 tbsp. dried rubbed sage
1 tsp. onion powder
1/2 cup shaved or grated parmesan cheese
2 eggs
1 1/4 cups chicken or veggie broth or stock

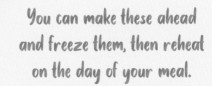

You can make these ahead and freeze them, then reheat on the day of your meal.

DIRECTIONS:

- Preheat oven to 350 degrees. Butter a 12-hole muffin tin.

- In a large skillet, crumble the sausage and cook until halfway done.

- Add the onions, mushrooms, and butter. Cook until tender.

- In a large mixing bowl, combine the crumbled cornbread and the sausage mixture. Add salt and pepper.

- Add the sage, onion powder, parmesan cheese, eggs, and broth. Mix with hands until all ingredients are moist but hold together.

- Using a 3-oz. ice-cream scoop, place 12 balls into the prepared muffin tin and pat tops flat.

- Bake for 30 minutes.

Sunday-Supper Green Beans and 'Maters

My mom would make traditional green beans and add home-canned tomatoes to them just before servin'. It was a dish that was handed down to her, but I swear neither one of us can remember who gave it to her. Anyway, it's mine now to twist. I've added an Italian flair with seasonin's and parmesan cheese. If y'all wanna hear somethin' really funny, you should hear me say "buono" with my Southern drawl.

Serves 4-6

INGREDIENTS:
4 tbsp. butter
1 pkg. dry Italian salad dressing
1 (14.5 oz.) can diced seasoned tomatoes
2 (14.5 oz.) cans cut green beans, drained
2 cups shredded parmesan cheese

GARNISH:
Shredded parmesan cheese

You can use any type of green bean you like.

DIRECTIONS:

- Preheat oven to 325 degrees. Butter an 11x7 casserole dish.

- In a skillet over medium heat, melt the butter and stir in the seasoning pack.

- Add the tomatoes and simmer for a few minutes.

- Add the green beans and stir; cook for 3-4 minutes.

- Place bean mixture in prepared dish and sprinkle the top with cheese.

- Bake for 30 minutes, or until bubbly and cheese just starts to brown around edges. Serve garnished with shredded cheese.

Super-Creamy Mac and Cheese Bake

Unfortunately, it has become a tradition to use an unnamed, very yellow, cheese product to make mac and cheese. Honey baby, sweetie pie, y'all ain't buyin' real cheese off the shelf at the local big-box store. My twist on mac and cheese is to make traditional mac and cheese, usin' real cheeses and a creamy béchamel sauce. My one extra twist to this recipe is to add just a touch of dry mustard. Trust me, it really does somethin' that takes mac and cheese up a notch.

Serves 8-10

INGREDIENTS:
1 lb. dried medium shell pasta
Olive oil
³⁄₄ cup butter
½ cup all-purpose flour
½ cup whole milk
2½ cups half-and-half
2 cups shredded sharp cheddar cheese
2 cups shredded mild cheddar cheese
2 cups shredded Colby Jack cheese
2 tsp. salt
1 tsp. ground black pepper
1 tsp. dry mustard

You can use your favorite melting cheeses.

DIRECTIONS:
- Preheat oven to 325 degrees. Grease a 9x13 baking dish.

- Bring a large pot of salted water to a boil. When boiling, add dried pasta and cook 2 minutes less than the package directions, for al dente. Drain and drizzle with a little bit of olive oil to keep from sticking.

- In a large saucepan over medium heat, melt butter. Sprinkle in flour and whisk to combine. Cook for approximately 1 minute, whisking often. Slowly pour in the milk and half-and-half, whisking constantly until combined and smooth.

- Continue to cook, whisking very often, until it reaches a very thick consistency.

- Combine all the cheeses and divide into 3 equal piles.

- Remove sauce from heat. Stir in spices and 1 pile cheese. Stir until completely melted and smooth.

- In a large mixing bowl, stir together the drained pasta and the cheese sauce until fully combined.

- Pour half of the pasta mixture into the prepared baking dish. Top with second pile of cheese, then top that with the remaining pasta mixture.

- Sprinkle the rest of the cheese over the top. Bake for 15 minutes, until cheese is bubbly and lightly golden brown.

Tasty Fried Turnips

Now I ain't gonna lie, turnips were one of my least favorite foods that were cooked in Granny's kitchen. They were just stewed with butter, and they didn't pass the palate test with me. One day I was talkin' with a friend and somehow, the subject of turnips came up. She tried to convince me that turnips could be tasty. I thought she'd bumped her head and bit her tongue off. But after she convinced me to try her fried turnips, I have to say I was shocked. Normally, I wouldn't have put a turnip recipe in the outhouse. But when I put my twist of sweet honey and chopped chives in a batch of fried turnips, I started makin' amends to every turnip I ever said a bad word about.

Serves 4-6

INGREDIENTS:

4 large turnips
3 tbsp. butter
2 tbsp. canola oil
2 tbsp. honey
Salt and ground black pepper to taste
¼ cup chopped chives

Always stir the turnips, to keep them from sticking.

DIRECTIONS:

- Wash turnips, trim off ends, cut in half lengthwise, and slice.

- In a large skillet over medium heat, add the butter and oil. When butter is melted, add the turnips. Place a lid on skillet, and cook for 5 minutes.

- After 5 minutes, remove lid and add the honey, salt, and pepper. Stir to combine, put lid back on, and cook for 8 minutes or until tender. Remove lid and allow to fry down, stirring occasionally.

- When turnips are slightly browned, transfer to a serving dish and sprinkle with chives.

Twice-Baked Sweet Taters

If you love a good sweet-tater casserole and a twice-baked tater, you're gonna love this twist. It's a sweet-tater casserole usin' the sweet tater as the casserole dish. Lord Honey, it'll make your eyes roll to the back of your brain.

Makes 4

INGREDIENTS:
4 medium sweet taters
2 tbsp. veggie oil
2 tsp. salt

FILLING:
1/2 cup butter, room temp
1/2 cup light brown sugar
1/4 tsp. salt
2 tsp. ground cinnamon
1 cup mini marshmallows
1 cup chopped pecans divided
3 tbsp. minced candied ginger

GLAZE:
1 cup balsamic vinegar
2 tbsp. honey
2 tbsp. bourbon (optional)

GARNISH:
4 strips bacon, cooked crispy and crumbled

Running short on time? Place taters in a microwave-proof dish, cover with cling wrap, and microwave around 10 minutes, or until tender.

DIRECTIONS:
- Preheat oven to 400 degrees. Line a baking sheet with foil.
- Wash and dry the sweet taters. Rub each with oil and sprinkle with salt. Bake for about 1 hour, or until tender.
- Remove and allow to cool for 25 minutes.
- To make the filling, combine butter, brown sugar, salt, and cinnamon.
- Stir in marshmallows, ¾ cup pecans, and candied ginger.
- In a saucepan over medium heat, bring the glaze ingredients to a boil. Cook until reduced and thick like molasses, about 15 minutes.
- Cut the potatoes open from end to end, without cutting all the way through. Push the ends toward each other to make a well for the filling.
- Top each potato with an equal amount of filling.
- Sprinkle the remaining pecans over the filling. Place potatoes back in oven and bake another 5 minutes or until the filling is bubbly.
- Transfer to a serving tray, sprinkle with crispy bacon, and drizzle with glaze.

Chapter 4

DINNER BELL'S RINGIN'
(MAINS)

Apple-Butter Ham Steaks

BBQ Meatball-Cornbread Bake

Best-Ever Steak Fingers

Cast-Iron Skillet Dinner Rolls

Benna's Crazy-Good Meatloaf

Cornmeal Hoecakes

Country Cornmeal Salmon Patties

Downhome Salisbury Steak

"Eye"-talian Stuffed Peppers

Firecracker Catfish with Fresh Corn Relish

Happy Hushpuppies

Lip-Smackin' Beef and Pickles

Oven-Fried Pork Ribs and Spicy Kraut

Papaw George's Oyster Dressin'

Savory Chicken Squares

Quick Chicken and Dumplin's

Roasted Chicken with Root Veggies

Peach and Sage Glazed Turkey Cutlets

Smothered Shrimp and Grits

Sweet and Spicy Pork Kabobs

Sweet Tea and Bourbon Fried Chicken

Red Beans and Rice

When I was growin' up, we really did ring a dinner bell to signal that the workday had ended and that dinner was ready. Lord Honey, I was happier than a *possum eatin' a sweet tater* just to know that we'd all be sittin' around the dinner table eatin' great food and sharin' stories.

Even though farm life and dinnertime have changed over the years, I hope that y'all will take the time to sit down at the dinner table with your family and friends and enjoy a home-cooked meal, even if it's just once a week.

From unique ingredients to easy prep, I think you will love these *twisted* dinner recipes that develop traditional flavors in less time.

Apple-Butter Ham Steaks

Apple butter is a staple in my family's kitchen. We used to make jars and jars of it in the fall so we could have it all year long. Ever'one knows that apples pair perfectly with ham. That's why I decided to add the twist of the warm, spicy flavors of apple butter with the savory taste of a good ham steak. This main dish is guaranteed to give y'all a hankerin' for ham.

Serves 4

INGREDIENTS:
2 ham steaks

GLAZE:
2 cups apple butter
½ cup apple juice
½ cup orange juice
2 tbsp. spicy brown mustard
2 tsp. Worcestershire sauce

This works great for leftover ham after the holidays.

DIRECTIONS:
- Preheat grill or grill pan to medium-high heat.

- In a mixing bowl, whisk glaze ingredients until well combined.

- Grill the ham steaks for 4-5 minutes. Flip steaks and glaze; cook another 5 minutes. Flip and glaze again. Continue this process approximately 3 more times, cooking each side for 2-3 minutes between turning. You want a nice caramelization.

- Transfer to a serving platter and serve.

BBQ Meatball-Cornbread Bake

BBQ meatballs are a mainstay at Southern celebrations like baby showers and birthday parties. I gave this party favorite an entrée twist by makin' it a one-pan meal, bread included.

Serves 8

INGREDIENTS:
1 lb. 80/20 ground beef
1 lb. mild breakfast sausage
½ cup oats
½ cup minced onion
2 tsp. garlic powder
½ cup grated parmesan cheese
2 eggs

BBQ SAUCE:
½ cup butter, room temp
¼ cup bacon drippings or canola oil
1 medium onion, grated
1 tbsp. yellow or Dijon mustard
½ cup brown sugar
¼ cup honey
2 cups ketchup
1 tbsp. Worcestershire sauce
½ cup apple juice
2 tsp. onion powder
2 tbsp. apple cider vinegar
1 tsp. garlic powder
2 tbsp. bourbon (optional)
2 tsp. salt
2 tsp. ground black pepper
1 tbsp. chili powder

This can also be made with ground turkey or ground chicken.

CORNBREAD TOPPING:
1 cup self-rising cornmeal
½ cup shredded cheddar cheese
½ cup milk
¼ cup water

DIRECTIONS:
- Preheat oven to 375 degrees. Grease a 9x13 baking dish or large cast-iron skillet with butter or nonstick cooking spray.

- In a bowl, mix meat, oats, onions, garlic powder, cheese, and eggs lightly with your hands, making sure not to overmix. Form walnut-size meatballs, place in the prepared dish, and bake for 20 minutes. Remove and make BBQ sauce.

- To make the BBQ sauce, in a saucepan over medium heat, melt the butter with the bacon drippings. Add the onion, and cook until tender. Add the rest of the sauce ingredients, reduce heat to low, and cook for 10 minutes or until slightly thickened. Pour over meatballs.

- In a medium mixing bowl, combine the cornbread topping ingredients. Pour batter over the BBQ-sauced meatballs. Bake for 30-35 minutes or until golden brown and bubbly.

Best-Ever Steak Fingers

Whether y'all call it country fried or chicken fried doesn't change the fact that this breaded and deep-fried piece of beef, slathered with gravy, is a Southern institution. How do you twist an institution? By turning it into chicken-fried steak fingers, of course. These are easy to pick up and easy to dip in my creamy dill sauce or a traditional country gravy. I mean, really, who doesn't like to eat a good finger ever' now and then, especially when it's deep fried?

Serves 6

INGREDIENTS:
Veggie oil for frying
2 cups all-purpose flour
2 tbsp. all-purpose steak seasoning, divided
1 cup buttermilk
1 egg
4 lb. beef cube steak

This is also good served with country gravy and biscuits.

DIPPING SAUCE:
1 cup mayo
½ cup sour cream
2 tbsp. yellow mustard
1 pkg. dry Italian salad dressing
2 tbsp. dried dill

DIRECTIONS:
- Preheat oven to lowest temperature.
- Pour 1 inch oil into a large cast-iron or other thick-bottomed skillet. Turn heat to medium low.
- Place the flour in a shallow pan. Sprinkle half the steak seasoning over flour, and mix together.
- Pour the milk and egg into another shallow pan and whisk together.
- Cut steak into 1-inch strips. Add the rest of the steak seasoning, rubbing into each piece.
- Turn heat to medium on skillet.
- Place each strip in the flour mix, then into the milk and egg mix, then back into the flour. Shake off excess and place each strip on a plate. Repeat until all strips are coated.
- Sprinkle a few drops flour over oil. If it sizzles, it's ready to fry.
- Using tongs or a fork, place strips side by side in hot oil. Don't crowd the pan, or it will cool the oil.
- After about 2-3 minutes, when strips start to brown on bottom, turn over. When second side is brown, remove and place on a cooling rack that has been set on a cookie sheet. Set the sheet in the preheated oven. Repeat until all fingers are cooked.
- In a bowl, whisk together all dipping sauce ingredients.

Cast-Iron Skillet Dinner Rolls

Ever'one in the South knows that it ain't a meal 'til the bread's on the table. It may not be considered good manners, but bread is our utensil of choice when it comes to gettin' ever' bit of food off our plates and ever' drop of juice outta our bowls. I mean, nothin' sops up potlikker like a soft, tender yeast roll. My twist on traditional yeast rolls is to add fresh herbs for extra flavor and potato flakes for extra tenderness and bake them in a cast-iron skillet for an extra-golden finish.

Serves 6

INGREDIENTS:

2 pkg. instant yeast
$\frac{3}{4}$ cup warm water
$\frac{1}{4}$ cup warm evaporated milk
$\frac{1}{4}$ cup honey
$\frac{1}{4}$ cup butter, melted, divided
1 tsp. salt
1 egg
2-3 cups all-purpose flour
$1\frac{1}{4}$ cups instant mashed-potato flakes
4 sprigs rosemary, stemmed and rough chopped

TOPPING:

$\frac{1}{2}$ cup melted butter
$\frac{1}{4}$ cup honey
1 tbsp. flaky sea salt for garnish

To check if the water and milk are at the right temperature, place a drop of each on your wrist. If they feel warm, then you are good to go.

DIRECTIONS:

- Preheat oven to 400 degrees. Butter a 12-inch cast-iron skillet.

- In a stand-mixer bowl, combine yeast, water, milk, and honey. Mix until yeast is dissolved. Let stand for 3 minutes. Then mix in half of the butter, the salt, and egg.

- Add 2 cups flour, the instant potatoes, and rosemary. Fit the mixer with a dough hook and, starting on low, mix until combined. If the dough is sticky, add another 1 cup flour and keep mixing. Dough will be slightly sticky but not super moist.

- When dough forms a ball, turn mixer to medium and let knead for 6 minutes.

- Remove dough. Divide into 12 equal pieces and shape into balls.

- Place in prepared skillet, cover with plastic wrap, and set in a warm area of the kitchen. Let rise for 20-22 minutes, or until the dough has doubled in size. Brush tops of rolls with remaining butter. Brush with a light hand; don't push down on rolls.

- Bake for 25-30 minutes. Then remove, brush with butter and honey, and sprinkle with flaky sea salt.

Benna's Crazy-Good Meatloaf

Benna is a nickname for my aunt Brenda. She makes the best old-fashioned meatloaf with just a few simple ingredients. Meatloaf isn't meant to be complicated. That's why my twist *on meatloaf is to keep it simple. I use old-fashioned oats as a binder and a few simple ingredients that add plenty of flavor and texture. Sometimes the KISS rule works best:* Keep It Simple Sweetie.

Serves 12

INGREDIENTS:
Nonstick cooking spray
3 lb. 96/4 ground beef
2 eggs
1 cup old-fashioned oats
3 tbsp. onion powder
¾ cup ketchup
¼ cup Worcestershire sauce
¼ cup steak sauce
2-3 tsp. ground white pepper
Salt to taste

TOPPING:
1½ cups ketchup
¾ cup light brown sugar

> If you use any type of beef below the 96/4, you will have to drain the grease off before the last 30 minutes of baking.

DIRECTIONS:
- Preheat oven to 400 degrees and spray a 9x13 baking dish with nonstick cooking spray.

- In a large mixing bowl, mix the next 8 ingredients lightly with your hands, making sure not to overmix.

- Place in the prepared dish and pat out flat. Sprinkle top with salt.

- In a small bowl, whisk together the topping ingredients. Spread evenly over top of meat mixture.

- Cover with foil and bake for 90 minutes. Remove foil, and bake another 30 minutes.

- Allow to cool for 10 minutes, then cut into squares and transfer to a serving tray.

Cornmeal Hoecakes

Hoecakes have a long tradition in the South. They get their name because they were literally cooked on the blade of a hoe over an open fire. Hoecakes are made from a very simple batter. In keepin' with the tradition of hoecakes, I've given y'all a traditional recipe. There's lots of ways y'all can put your own twists on hoecakes, such as addin' herbs, onions, bacon, or cheese.

Serves 4

INGREDIENTS:
²⁄₃ cup canola oil
1½ cups white or yellow self-rising cornmeal
²⁄₃ cup full-fat buttermilk
1 egg
Soft butter for serving

To make other variations, you can add whole-kernel corn, chopped jalapenos, cooked crumbled bacon, sliced green onions, or shredded cheese to the batter.

DIRECTIONS:

- Heat the oil in a skillet over medium heat.

- In a mixing bowl, combine the meal, buttermilk, and egg. Sometimes you may need to add a touch of water to make it pourable.

- Drop by spoonful into hot oil. Brown hoecakes on both sides, and transfer to a paper-towel-lined plate. Continue frying until all batter is gone.

- Serve with butter.

Country Cornmeal Salmon Patties

Salmon patties, using canned salmon, date back to the Great Depression in helping families stretch their food budget and put protein in their diets. Thank goodness they became ingrained in the Southern food culture and are still around today as an affordable way to put a tasty meal on the table. I think of salmon patties as country folks' twisted version of a crab cake.

Makes 6 patties

INGREDIENTS:

1 cup canola or veggie oil

1 (14¾ oz.) can salmon, drained

½ cup self-rising cornmeal

1 egg

¼ tsp. salt

½ tsp. ground black pepper

¼ tsp. onion powder

½ tsp. dill

2 tbsp. mayo

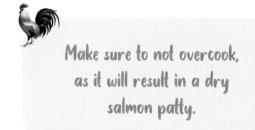

Make sure to not overcook, as it will result in a dry salmon patty.

DIRECTIONS:

- Heat the oil in a cast-iron or nonstick skillet over medium heat for 3-4 minutes.

- In a mixing bowl, flake the salmon up with a fork. Add the cornmeal, egg, salt, pepper, onion powder, dill, and mayo; stir to combine.

- Using your hands, divide into 6 balls and pat out into patties.

- Fry in hot oil on each side for 4-5 minutes or until brown and crispy.

- Transfer to a paper-towel-lined plate to drain.

Downhome Salisbury Steak

Lordy, I feel sorry for folks that think Salisbury steak only comes from a foil pan in the freezer section of the supermarket. Remember to pray for those folks on Sunday. Speakin' of Sunday, I loved when we had homemade Salisbury steak as our after-church family dinner. My twist on traditional Salisbury steak is to chock it full of flavor and top it with a rich, mushroom gravy.

Serves 4

INGREDIENTS:

Nonstick cooking spray
1 lb. lean ground beef
1 medium onion, minced
1 pkg. dry brown gravy mix
1 egg
2 tbsp. steak sauce (A-1)
1 tbsp. Worcestershire sauce
2 tsp. all-purpose steak seasoning

GRAVY:

1 pkg. dry mushroom gravy mix
1 1/2 cups warm water
2 tsp. Worcestershire sauce
1 (6 oz.) jar sliced mushrooms, drained

This can be made with any ground meat.

DIRECTIONS:

- Preheat oven to 350 degrees. Spray a 9x13 baking dish with nonstick cooking spray.

- In a mixing bowl, lightly combine the beef, onion, gravy mix, egg, sauces, and seasoning.

- Divide into 4 equal balls, pat into patties, and place in prepared dish.

- To make the gravy, in same bowl, whisk gravy mix, water, and Worcestershire sauce. Pour over patties. Layer mushrooms evenly over the top.

- Cover and bake for 45-60 minutes, until patties are tender and gravy is thick.

- Bake, uncovered, another 5-7 minutes.

- Transfer patties to a serving platter and drizzle the pan gravy over the top.

"Eye"-talian Stuffed Peppers

My Granny Jean made the best stuffed cabbage rolls, full of pork and beef, peppers, and onions and smothered in home-canned tomato juice. One thing about old-time cookin' is that it didn't have a variety of herbs, because they just weren't easily available. So, I've taken Granny Jean's stuffin' recipe and given it an Italian twist by addin' Italian sausage, herbs, and cheeses. Now, I've taken some flak for my pronunciation of the word "Italian" on national television, but honey, that's just how I talk. I mean, it just comes outta my mouth as "Eye"-talian, and Lord knows my brain don't stop long enough to let my mouth catch up.

Serves 6

INGREDIENTS:

Nonstick cooking spray
1 lb. mild Italian sausage
1 cup diced white button mushrooms
1 small onion, minced
1 (15 oz.) can diced tomatoes
4 cloves garlic, minced
1 tbsp. dried basil
2 tsp. dried oregano
¼ tsp. crushed red pepper flakes
1 cup grated parmesan cheese, divided
Salt and ground black pepper to taste
3 bell peppers, any color, cut in half lengthwise, stemmed and seeded
1 cup grated mozzarella cheese
6 slices provolone cheese
½ cup parsley for garnish

> You can also make this with ground beef or ground turkey.

DIRECTIONS:

- Preheat oven to 350 degrees. Spray a 9x9 baking dish with nonstick cooking spray.

- In a medium skillet, brown and crumble the sausage.

- Add the mushrooms and onions and cook for 10 minutes.

- Add the tomatoes, garlic, basil, oregano, and red pepper flakes. Stir to combine, and cook for 5 minutes. Remove from heat.

- Stir in half of the parmesan cheese; salt and pepper to taste.

- Place the 6 pepper halves in prepared baking dish.

- Fill each pepper half with sausage mixture. Spoon any leftover sausage mixture around peppers.

- Bake for 30 minutes.

- Remove from oven, and sprinkle remaining parmesan cheese and the mozzarella over the top. Place 1 slice provolone over each pepper half.

- Return to oven to allow cheese to melt; this will take about 6-8 minutes.

- Transfer to a serving platter and garnish with parsley.

Firecracker Catfish with Fresh Corn Relish

Fried catfish is as country as Hee Haw. *My* twist *on this country catch is to give it a lot of heat with a spicy breadin' and dippin' sauce, and then cool it down with a fresh and flavorful corn relish. This was one of my signature dishes that the judges loved on* Food Network Star.

Serves 4

INGREDIENTS:

²⁄₃ cup all-purpose flour
²⁄₃ cup yellow cornmeal
2 tsp. salt
½ tsp. ground black pepper
¾ tsp. cayenne pepper
½ tsp. lemon pepper seasoning
½ cup buttermilk
1 egg
1 tbsp. hot sauce
1 tbsp. Old Bay Seasoning
4 large catfish fillets
Veggie oil for frying

If you don't like real spicy food, adjust the amount of spices.

FRESH CORN RELISH:

6 ears fresh corn, kernels cut off
½ bunch green onions, sliced
1 pt. mixed cherry tomatoes, cut in half
¼ cup chopped fresh dill
Juice of 2 limes
¼ cup olive oil
1 tbsp. honey
2 tsp. wholegrain mustard
1 tsp. garlic powder
Salt and ground black pepper to taste

FIRECRACKER SAUCE:

1 cup mayo
2 tbsp. hot sauce
1 tsp. chili powder
½ tsp. ground white pepper

DIRECTIONS:

- In a zip-top bag, shake flour, cornmeal, salt, pepper, cayenne, and lemon pepper until combined.

- In a mixing bowl, whisk together buttermilk, egg, hot sauce, and Old Bay Seasoning.

- Place the catfish in a zip-top bag and add the buttermilk mixture. Seal and put in the fridge for 2 hours.

- Drop 1 fish fillet into the cornmeal breading and shake bag lightly to liberally coat. Place coated fish on a baking sheet. Repeat with remaining fillets.

- While coating sets, pour 3 inches oil into a Dutch oven and heat over medium-high heat.

- Fry fish until golden brown on one side, then flip and cook until other side is golden brown; this takes about 4 minutes per side. Transfer to a paper-towel-lined platter to drain.

- While fish is frying, make the relish. In a bowl, toss the corn, onions, tomatoes, and dill to combine.

- In a jar with a lid, shake the lime juice, oil, honey, mustard, and spices until combined. Pour over corn mixture and toss.

- Place the firecracker sauce ingredients in a bowl and whisk together. Pour into a zip-top bag and lay in the fridge until ready to serve.

- Once all the fish is fried, spread the corn relish on a serving platter and lay the fish on top. Make a small cut in the corner of the zip-top bag that the sauce is in, and drizzle the sauce over the fish.

Happy Hushpuppies

Where I come from, if there's fish, there's gonna be hushpuppies. The perfect hushpuppy needs to have a touch of sweetness and a hint of onion and be tender on the inside and golden and crunchy on the outside. I can't mess with perfection, so my twist on hushpuppies is to make 'em happy with a sweet, creamy honey butter. Y'all will love these as much as a puppy loves a shoe.

Serves 6-8

INGREDIENTS:
4 cups self-rising white cornmeal
2 tbsp. white sugar
¼ cup minced onion
2 eggs
2 cups whole buttermilk
8 tbsp. cold water
Veggie oil for frying

You can freeze these for later and then heat up again.

HONEY BUTTER:
2 cups very soft butter
¼ cup honey
2 tbsp. powdered sugar

DIRECTIONS:
- In a large mixing bowl, stir the cornmeal and sugar together.

- In another mixing bowl, place onions. Add eggs and buttermilk, and beat until frothy.

- Pour the mixture into the meal and stir lightly to mix.

- Add just enough of the cold water to make the dough have a biscuit-dough consistency.

- Pour 3 inches oil into a Dutch oven and heat to 350 degrees, as measured by a cooking thermometer. Drop about 5-6 dough balls into the hot oil and fry until golden brown; remove and transfer to a paper-towel-lined plate.

- Repeat frying until all dough is gone.

- Place the honey butter ingredients in a bowl and whisk together.

Lip-Smackin' Beef and Pickles

The twist to this recipe is in the name–I mean, really, who's gonna smack their lips at eatin' a piece of beef rolled around a dill pickle? Well, don't be surprised if, after y'all try this, your lips don't start smackin' ever'time you hear the words beef and pickles in the same sentence. I was skeptical too when my friend Harriette said she was makin' me her version of a German dish called Rouladen, especially when I saw those pickles. Well, needless to say, my lips were smackin', and it wasn't the last time she made it for me.

Serves 6

INGREDIENTS:

1 lb. thinly sliced round steak

½ cup yellow mustard

1 medium onion, minced

12 dill pickle spears

2 cans (10.5 oz.) beef consommé soup

Salt and ground black pepper to taste

1 tbsp. cornstarch

2 tbsp. water

You can use spicy brown mustard for a kick.

DIRECTIONS:

- Preheat oven to 350 degrees.

- Cut the steak into 12 equal pieces. Spread a thin layer of mustard over each piece of steak, and sprinkle with onions.

- Lay a pickle spear at edge of 1 beef piece and roll up. Secure with toothpick. Repeat until all the steak has been used.

- In a skillet, add a touch of oil or butter, and brown each steak roll. Transfer to a Dutch oven, and pour beef consommé soup over the top. Salt and pepper to taste.

- Put on lid, and bake until tender, about 45-60 minutes. Remove from oven.

- Mix the cornstarch and water together and add to the pot to thicken the broth.

Oven-Fried Pork Ribs and Spicy Kraut

When we hear the word "ribs" in the South, we automatically think of smoked meat slathered in BBQ sauce. Well, my twist on baby-back ribs is to bread 'em like fried chicken and oven-bake 'em 'til they're nice and crunchy on the outside and fork-tender to the cut. I grew up eatin' pork and kraut together, so it's no stretch for me to pair my ribs with some tangy, spicy kraut. All you need is a big pone of cornbread and a slice of fresh onion to make this pork-a-licious platter a new dinnertime fave.

Serves 6-8

INGREDIENTS:
$\frac{1}{2}$ cup mayo
2 cups whole buttermilk
1 egg
1 tbsp. smoked paprika
1 tsp. salt
$\frac{1}{2}$ tsp. ground black pepper
2 racks baby-back pork ribs
3 cups panko breadcrumbs
1 cup yellow cornmeal
$\frac{1}{2}$ cup grated parmesan cheese

SPICY KRAUT:
3 tbsp. bacon drippings or butter
1 (32 oz.) bag kraut, undrained
2 jalapenos, seeded and diced

This can also be made with pork chops.

DIRECTIONS:
- Preheat oven to 375 degrees. Line a baking sheet with parchment paper.

- In a large bowl, mix mayo, buttermilk, egg, paprika, salt, and pepper.

- Cut rib racks into individual ribs, then place them in the buttermilk mixture.

- In a shallow bowl, combine the panko, cornmeal, and cheese.

- Roll each rib in the panko mixture, and place in a single layer on prepared baking sheet.

- Bake for 40 minutes. Remove baking sheet, turn ribs over, and bake another 20 minutes.

- While ribs are baking, make the spicy kraut. In a skillet over medium heat, place bacon drippings or butter. Add the kraut and jalapenos, reduce heat to low, and cook for 25-30 minutes, or until all liquid is gone.

- When ribs are done, let them rest for 10 minutes.

- Transfer the kraut to a serving platter, and top with the ribs.

Papaw George's Oyster Dressin'

Papaw George was the one who always made the dressin' when I was growin' up. It was a sure thing at Thanksgivin' and a special treat durin' the summer, when we'd have a wild-game dinner. A lot of folks may think it's a twist to use oysters in dressin', but it's actually a tradition that dates to the British colonies, where oysters were easy pickin's along the shoreline. As the country progressed inland, it wasn't an easy ingredient to get, but with cannin' and fish markets, oyster dressin' soon found its way to those Thanksgivin' tables. Now don't be turned off by the sound of it—it's really not fishy and is a great way to add moisture and texture to a holiday classic. For me, it's a special way to remember Papaw George and my family gathered 'round the Thanksgivin' table.

Serves 6-8

INGREDIENTS:

½ cup chopped celery
½ cup chopped onions
½ cup butter, melted
3 cups bread cubes
3 cups crumbled cornbread
3 eggs, beaten
1 pt. oysters, undrained
2 cups turkey or chicken broth
2 tbsp. butter

Leftover oyster dressin' makes a great sandwich.

DIRECTIONS:

- Preheat oven to 350 degrees. Butter an 11x7 casserole dish.

- In a large skillet, sauté the celery and onions in the melted butter until tender.

- In a large mixing bowl, place the bread cubes and cornbread. Add the eggs, oysters, and sautéed vegetables, and stir to combine.

- Add enough broth to moisten. You don't want it soupy. Begin with a little and add as needed.

- Pour into prepared casserole dish and dot the top with butter.

- Bake for 30-40 minutes, or until edges start to brown.

Savory Chicken Squares

This recipe was given to me by one of my best friends, Nicole, who got it from her mom, Jeanne, who got it from a friend. I love it when a recipe travels around like that. Passin' down recipes is a tradition that connects generations of family and friends. The twist here is to keep the tradition alive, passin' recipes to y'all and hopin' you just keep passin' 'em down the line. This is a quick and easy recipe full of flavor and wrapped in a crescent roll. What else could you want on a hectic weeknight when tryin' to plan a tasty dinner that ever'one will love? Trust me, y'all will keep this one in your back pocket as a go-to that pleases ever'one.

Serves 4

INGREDIENTS:

3 oz. cream cheese, room temp
3 tbsp. butter, soft
2 cups cubed cooked chicken
½ tsp. salt
½ tsp. ground black pepper
2 tbsp. whole milk
1 tbsp. minced onion
1 tbsp. chopped pimentos
1 (8 oz.) tube refrigerated crescent-roll dough
1 tbsp. butter, melted
¾ cup crushed seasoned croutons

This is good with leftover turkey.

DIRECTIONS:

- Preheat oven to 350 degrees. Set aside an ungreased cookie sheet.

- In a mixing bowl, mix cream cheese and soft butter until smooth. Add the next 6 ingredients and mix.

- Separate the dough into 4 rectangles, pressing seams together.

- Spoon ½ cup chicken mixture onto middle of each crescent square.

- Bring the 4 corners of each square up over filling, and twist together to seal.

- Brush tops with melted butter and dip in the crushed croutons. Transfer to ungreased cookie sheet.

- Bake for 20-25 minutes until golden brown.

Quick Chicken and Dumplin's

Lord Honey, a 100 percent fact of life is that there is nothin' more Southern than a big pot of chicken and dumplin's. This was one of the first meals I had my Grandma Creech teach me to make. It took a mighty long time from start to finish to have my favorite comfort food of all time on the table. I think that's one of the reasons folks are intimidated about makin' chicken and dumplin's. My twist on this number-one Southern classic is to make it quicker and easier but keep all the warm, yummy, comfort flavors that we've come to expect from traditional chicken and dumplin's. Let me tell y'all, this really will make a tomcat lick a kitten.

Serves 4

INGREDIENTS:
1 rotisserie chicken
1 (32 oz.) box chicken broth
2 cans cream of chicken soup
1/2 cup butter
1/2 tsp. ground white pepper

DUMPLIN'S:
2 1/2 cups biscuit baking mix
4 tbsp. butter, melted
1/3 cup whole milk
1/3 cup chicken broth

GARNISH:
Chopped fresh parsley

Never stir dumplings. Always push them; this keeps them from breaking up.

DIRECTIONS:

- Pull the chicken off the bone and cut into cubes.

- In a large Dutch oven, add the chicken broth, cream of chicken soup, and butter. Turn to medium heat, and bring to a slow boil. Then add the pepper and chicken. Bring to a full boil.

- In a mixing bowl, stir the dumplin's ingredients until combined; the dough should be the texture of drop biscuits.

- When broth is boiling, drop dough into broth using a teaspoon. Make sure to use all the dough; you may have to push the dough around to find spots.

- Once all of the dough is in, put on lid and reduce heat to low. Cook for 5-10 minutes. Transfer chicken and dumplin's to a serving dish, and sprinkle with chopped parsley.

Roasted Chicken with Root Veggies

Chicken is the most consumed meat in the United States, but it goes without sayin' that we can't have it fried seven days a week. Roastin' chicken, usin' spices and veggies as aromatics, is an awesome way to enjoy this flavorful bird, with the added twist of making it a light and healthy meal.

Serves 6-8

INGREDIENTS:

3 tbsp. fresh thyme, minced
4 cloves garlic, minced
Zest of 1 lemon
1 tsp. ground white pepper
1 tsp. salt
1 tsp. onion powder
¼ cup olive oil
½ cup butter, melted
1 tbsp. lemon juice
3-4 parsnips, peeled, cut into ½-inch-thick rounds
3-4 carrots, peeled, cut into ½-inch-thick rounds
4 medium turnips, cut into wedges
4-6 golden potatoes, cut into wedges
1 large sweet tater, peeled and cubed
4-6 chicken breasts, skin on
2-3 sprigs thyme

You can also place the ingredients in a slow cooker in the same layered fashion and cook on high for 3 hours, then remove chicken and brown under broiler.

DIRECTIONS:

- Preheat oven to 375 degrees. Spray or butter a large baking dish.

- In a mixing bowl, stir minced thyme, garlic, lemon zest, pepper, salt, onion powder, olive oil, butter, and lemon juice until combined.

- Place all the vegetables in the prepared baking dish. Sprinkle with a little salt.

- Place chicken breasts on top of vegetables, skin side up.

- Pour the spice oil mixture over the chicken and vegetables.

- Throw in the sprigs of thyme and cover with foil.

- Bake for 1 hour or until chicken is tender.

- Remove foil and bake another 20-25 minutes or until chicken and veggies start to brown.

Peach and Sage Glazed Turkey Cutlets

Turkey is such a versatile meat. It shouldn't just be bought at the deli for sandwiches or roasted once a year for Thanksgivin'. I love turkey and look for different ways to put it on my dinner table year round. This twist on turkey stays true to the flavors of the holidays but has an extra-sweet touch with a yummy peach glaze. Remember, y'all don't have to wait 'til Thanksgivin' to gobble 'til ya wobble.

Serves 6

INGREDIENTS:
2 large turkey cutlets
2 tsp. salt
1 tsp. ground black pepper

PEACH AND SAGE GLAZE:
1 (18 oz.) jar peach preserves
3 tbsp. butter, melted
Juice of ½ lemon
1 tbsp. Worcestershire sauce
2 tsp. garlic powder
2 tbsp. rubbed sage

GARNISH:
Fresh sage sprigs
Toasted pecans

> If you can't find turkey cutlets, you can use 6 large chicken breasts.

DIRECTIONS:
- Preheat oven to 375 degrees. Butter or spray a large baking dish.
- Add the turkey cutlets to the prepared baking dish and prick with a fork. Sprinkle with salt and pepper.
- In a mixing bowl, mix the glaze ingredients. Reserve ¼ cup.
- Brush turkey liberally with about half the glaze. Cover with foil and bake for 45 minutes. Remove foil and brush with the rest of the glaze. Bake another 20-25 minutes. Turkey is done when a meat thermometer reads 165 degrees.
- When turkey is done, remove from oven, cover with foil, and let stand for 20 minutes.
- On a cutting board, slice into 2-inch-thick slices. Transfer to a serving platter and drizzle with reserved glaze. Garnish with sage sprigs and pecans.

Smothered Shrimp and Grits

Where I came from, grits were considered a breakfast food. It wasn't 'til I traveled to the Low Country of South Carolina as an adult and got my first taste of shrimp and grits that I realized grits weren't just for breakfast anymore. Since then, I eat shrimp and grits anytime they're on the menu. I've put my twist on this Low Country classic by addin' the smoky flavor of gouda and toppin' it with a rich and creamy, mushroom-laden sauce. My good friend Lisa has marked this as one of her favorite Country Bling creations.

Serves 4

INGREDIENTS:
2 cups chicken or veggie stock
1/2 cup half-and-half
1/4 cup water
3/4 cup yellow or white grits, not quick cook
1/4 tsp. salt
1/2 tsp. ground black pepper
1 tsp. garlic powder
1/2 tsp. onion powder
8 tbsp. butter, divided
1 cup shredded smoked gouda or white cheddar
1 lb. shrimp, peeled and deveined
1 tbsp. seafood seasoning
2 tbsp. bacon drippings
1/2 cup minced onion
2 cups chopped mushrooms
1 clove garlic, minced
Juice of 1/2 lemon

GARNISH:
1 cup crumbled bacon

If you don't like shrimp, you can use cubed chicken.

DIRECTIONS:
- In a stockpot over medium heat, stir together the first 8 ingredients and 6 tbsp. butter. Bring to a boil, still over medium heat. Reduce heat to low and cook until thick, stirring often to keep from sticking.

- When grits are thick, stir in cheese.

- In a bowl, toss the shrimp in the seafood seasoning until coated.

- In a skillet over medium heat, melt the rest of the butter with the bacon drippings.

- Add the onions, mushrooms, and garlic and cook until onions are soft.

- Add the shrimp and cook for 3 minutes. Add lemon juice, and stir another minute.

- Ladle grits into 4 bowls. Divide the shrimp-mushroom mixture among the bowls and spoon the remaining sauce from the skillet over each. Sprinkle with cooked, crispy bacon crumbles.

Sweet and Spicy Pork Kabobs

Durin' the summer, I spend a lot of time grillin' and smokin' our meals. I love makin' kabobs, almost as much as I love sayin' the word "kabobs." I mean, face it, it's a funny word. There are endless ways to twist a kabob, from the meat you choose, to the unlimited choices of fruits and veggies. So go crazy with kabobs. This recipe only has three ingredients, but once y'all rub them with my spice list and glaze them with my tangy, sweet, bourbon sauce, these kabobs are gonna knock your socks off.

Serves 4

INGREDIENTS:
2 large sweet taters, peeled, cut into 1-inch cubes
2 lb. boneless pork loin chops, cut into 2-inch pieces
1 large sweet onion, cut into 1½-inch chunks and layers separated
8 (12 inch) bamboo or metal skewers

SPICE RUB:
4 tbsp. olive oil
1 tsp. onion powder
2 tsp. garlic powder
2 tsp. chili powder
1 tsp. salt
1 tsp. ground black pepper
¼ tsp. crushed red pepper flakes
½ tsp. ground sage

GLAZE:
2 tbsp. brown or Dijon mustard
6 tbsp. honey
2 tbsp. bourbon

> If using bamboo skewers, soak in water for 30 minutes first, to prevent burning.

DIRECTIONS:
- In a small saucepan, place tater pieces into a small saucepan and add just enough water to cover the tops. Bring to a boil over medium-high heat, when boiling, set your timer to 5 minutes, and cook until taters are nearly done, but still firm. Immediately drain and transfer to a bowl to cool.

- In a small mixing bowl, mix the spice rub ingredients.

- In a separate bowl, whisk together the glaze ingredients. Set aside.

- Toss pork with half of the spice mixture. Divide the rest of the spice mixture between the taters and onions and toss gently to combine.

- Thread the pork, sweet taters, and onions onto the skewers. You should have approximately 8 skewers.

- Brush the skewers with half of the glaze.

- Preheat grill to medium heat. Grill the pork skewers, turning frequently, for about 8 minutes, or until pork is cooked through.

- Remove from grill and brush on the rest of the glaze.

Sweet Tea and Bourbon Fried Chicken

Yes, yes, yes, three of my favorite things in the world, all twisted into one recipe. I mean, how could I represent the South and my home state of Kentucky any better than with sweet tea, bourbon, and fried chicken? Like my very good friend Lisa says, the only trick is not to drink all the sweet tea and bourbon before y'all get started. Good luck with that!

Serves 4-6

INGREDIENTS:
2 lb. bone-in chicken pieces, skin on, white and/or dark meat
Veggie oil for frying

SWEET TEA SOAK:
1 cup buttermilk
1 cup sweet Southern tea
¼ cup bourbon
2 eggs
1 tbsp. hot sauce
1 tsp. garlic powder
2 tsp. onion powder
1 tsp. poultry seasoning or ground sage
1 tsp. ground black pepper
2 tsp. salt

The soak and coating in this recipe work great on pork chops as well.

COATING:
2 cups self-rising cornmeal
½ cup all-purpose or self-rising flour
1 tsp. onion powder
½ tsp. garlic powder
1 tsp. ground black pepper
½ tsp. salt

DIRECTIONS:
- Place the chicken in a large bowl with a lid or a gallon-size zip-top bag.
- In a mixing bowl, stir the soak ingredients until combined. Pour over chicken and put in the fridge overnight or up to 48 hours.
- Preheat oven to 325 degrees.
- In a shallow dish, toss together the coating ingredients.
- In a large, heavy-bottomed pot, pour oil about 3 inches deep. Heat to 360 degrees, as measured by a cooking thermometer.
- Roll each piece of chicken in coating mix and place on a baking sheet.
- Place 3-4 pieces of chicken in oil, starting with any dark meat, because it takes longer to cook. Cook until medium brown or meat thermometer reads 165 degrees.
- Remove from oil and place on another baking sheet. Keep warm in oven.
- Continue this process until all chicken is fried.
- Serve hot with your favorite side dishes.

Red Beans and Rice

Red beans and rice come to us by way of New Orleans' Creole cuisine. It was traditionally eaten on Mondays, which was washing day, so the beans could be put on to cook all day. It also probably made use of ham and hambones left over from a big Sunday dinner. Even though some folks serve it as a side, it is really considered a one-pot meal, like jambalaya or gumbo. My twist on this NOLA tradition is to save time by starting with canned beans instead of dried, and then chock the beans full of flavor with meat, veggies, spices, and, yes, even beer. Y'all will be singin' "On the Bayou" after you get a taste of this Creole classic.

Serves 4-6

INGREDIENTS:

1 pkg. polish sausage, sliced
1 medium onion, diced
1 rib celery, minced
1 carrot, diced
4 tbsp. light brown sugar
$\frac{1}{2}$ tsp. garlic powder
$\frac{1}{8}$ tsp. cayenne pepper
$\frac{1}{2}$ tsp. chili powder
$\frac{1}{2}$ tsp. Worcestershire sauce
12 oz. can light beer
16 oz. can red beans
Steamed white or brown rice
Hot sauce (optional)

This recipe freezes well.

DIRECTIONS:

- In a deep skillet over medium heat, cook sliced sausage for 5 minutes.

- Add the onion, celery, and carrot and cook for 8 minutes, stirring often.

- Add sugar, spices, Worcestershire sauce, beer, and beans and stir. Bring to a boil, and cook for 6 minutes. Reduce heat to simmer, and cook down until the liquid is gravy-like.

- Serve over steamed white or brown rice. Add a dash of hot sauce if desired.

162

LORD HONEY

Chapter 5

Lip-Smackin', Tongue-Slappin' Sweets (Desserts)

Aunt Mae's Oatmeal Cake

Award-Winnin' 7-Minute Frostin'

Bourbon Bread Puddin'

Bacon-Bourbon Pecan Pie

Blueberry-Lemon Hand Pies

Bourbon-Cherry Mousse Jars

Easy Appalachian Stack Cake

Butterscotch-Apple Crisp

Crunchy Peanut Butter Cookie Sammies

Must-Have Custard Pie with 7-Minute Meringue

Granny Creech's Cushaw Pie

Hummingbird Tart

Kentucky Bourbon Cake with Chocolate Ganache

New-South 'Nanner Puddin' Trifle

Orange-Slice Blondies

Pistachio Ice-Cream Delight

Out-of-This-World Cake

Pap's Southern Blackberry Cake

Scrumptious Sweet-Tater Bars

Snowdrop Cookies

Tried-and-True Piecrust

Southern Coconut Layered Sheet Cake

To-Die-For Chocolate-Mayo Cupcakes

True-South Sweet Tea Bundt Cake

"No thanks, I don't want dessert," said no Southerner ever! To be honest, though, we may not eat dessert at the end of a meal. Lord Honey, sometimes we eat dessert as our meal. It's just part of the Southern DNA to have a sweet tooth. It's not unusual to end breakfast with honey or jam on a biscuit, have a cookie or two after lunch, and, if a bona-fide dessert ain't fixed for after dinner, simply slather some molasses and butter on bread.

I would have to say that I have always had a "sweet spot" for makin' desserts. It really touches my inner child and takes me back to when my mom and aunts would spend hours in the kitchen makin' candies, cookies, cakes, and pies. We didn't have to have a special occasion to have a sweet treat. Dinner was special occasion enough.

Let me tell y'all, my *twisted* sweets will surely *make your tongue slap your brains out, wantin' more.*

Aunt Mae's Oatmeal Cake

Country cooks have always known that oats aren't just for breakfast. Even though a big, ol' bowl of sweet, hearty oatmeal is usually the first thing that comes to mind, oats can be used in all kinds of ways, from serving as a binder in foods such as meatloaf or stuffed peppers to adding texture in cookies and cakes. My aunt Mae's twist on this traditional breakfast staple was to make extra when she was cookin' breakfast for Uncle Bob, so she'd be sure to have some left over to make this moist, tender, coconut-topped cake. My own twist is to enhance the warm, cinnamon flavor with a li'l kick of ground ginger.

Serves 12

INGREDIENTS:
Nonstick cooking spray
1 cup quick-cook oats
1¼ cups boiling water
½ cup butter
1 cup white sugar
1 cup brown sugar, packed
2 eggs
1 tsp. vanilla
1⅓ cups self-rising flour
1 tsp. ground cinnamon
½ tsp. ground ginger

TOPPING:
4 tbsp. butter, melted
4 tbsp. canned evaporated milk
1 cup brown sugar, packed
1 cup flaked coconut

> Do not overmix the batter. It will make a gummy cake.

DIRECTIONS:

- Preheat oven to 350 degrees. Spray a 9x13 baking pan with nonstick cooking spray.

- Place oats in a small bowl, and pour the hot water over them. Let stand for 20 minutes.

- In a mixing bowl, cream the butter and sugars.

- Add oats to butter, and stir to combine.

- Add the eggs and vanilla, and stir to combine.

- Stir in the flour, cinnamon, and ginger.

- Pour batter into prepared baking pan. Bake for 45 minutes or until a toothpick inserted in the middle comes out clean.

- In a mixing bowl, stir all the topping ingredients together until combined.

- Spread over cake.

- Place under the broiler, with door ajar, and broil until it is medium brown.

Award-Winnin' 7-Minute Frostin'

This is the recipe that I used on my championship cake during a holiday baking competition. It is so fluffy, ooey, gooey, and pillowy soft that y'all could get lost in it like a big ol' fat cloud. It's perfect for icin' about any cake you come across. My twist on this award-winnin' frostin' is to use it as meringue on my pies and as fluff in my cookie sandwiches. It can be eaten plain or popped under the broiler for a traditional meringue finish. Trust me, y'all will be singin' the high praises of this heavenly creation.

Makes 4-5 cups

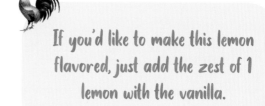

INGREDIENTS:

¾ cup + 2 tbsp. white sugar, divided

1 tbsp. light corn syrup

4 tbsp. water

3 egg whites

½ tsp. cream of tartar

¼ tsp. salt

1 tbsp. vanilla

If you'd like to make this lemon flavored, just add the zest of 1 lemon with the vanilla.

DIRECTIONS:

- In a saucepan over medium heat, stir together the ¾ cup sugar, corn syrup, and water until sugar is dissolved. Bring to a boil, still over medium heat. Once boiling, do not stir; boil for 5 minutes, or until it reads 230 degrees on a candy thermometer.

- In a stand-mixer bowl, place the egg whites, cream of tartar, and salt. Turn mixer to high, and beat until medium peaks form; this takes about 2 minutes. Then add the 2 tbsp. sugar and the vanilla, and whip until stiff peaks form, about another 1 minute.

- With mixer on low, stream the hot syrup into the stiff egg whites.

- Once all the syrup is in, turn mixer to high and beat for 7 minutes, or until frosting is cooled.

- Place in a piping bag or gallon-size zip-top bag for use on your dessert.

Bourbon Bread Puddin'

Bread puddin' dates back centuries as a way to utilize leftover bread. There are as many varieties of bread puddin' as Carter *has liver pills, rangin' from sweet to savory to somewhere in between. Because bread is such a mainstay on the Southern country table, there is usually an abundance of leftovers. Y'all know by now that bourbon is one of my favorite ways to* twist *tradition, so I'm sure it doesn't surprise anyone that I've added more than a shot of my go-to booze.*

Serves 10-12

This puddin' is great warm or at room temp. Serve with ice cream and candied pecans.

INGREDIENTS:
4-6 baked biscuits, cubed
4 large bagels, cubed
1/2 French baguette, cubed
Nonstick cooking spray
3/4 cup water
1/2 cup apple cider or apple juice
2 cups powdered plain coffee creamer
1/2 cup butter, melted
3 eggs
1 cup brown sugar, packed
2 tsp. ground cinnamon
2 tsp. ground ginger
3/4 cup bourbon
1 tbsp. vanilla

NUT TOPPING:
1 cup pecans, chopped
1 cup walnuts, chopped
1 tbsp. bourbon
1/2 tsp. ground cinnamon
1/2 cup butter, melted
Pinch of salt

BOURBON SAUCE:
1 cup butter
1/4 cup maple syrup
1 1/2 cups brown sugar
1 1/2 cups heavy cream
1/2 cup apple cider or apple juice
1/2 cup + 2 tbsp. bourbon, divided
Pinch of salt
2 tsp. vanilla

DIRECTIONS:
- Preheat oven to 350 degrees.
- Place the bread in a 9x13 baking pan that has been sprayed with nonstick cooking spray.
- In a mixing bowl, mix remaining pudding ingredients until well combined.
- Pour over bread, and smush with your hands until bread is moistened.
- Let stand while making nut topping.
- In a bowl, combine the topping ingredients. Sprinkle over bread mixture.
- Cover bread with foil and bake for 30-35 minutes. Remove foil and bake another 25 minutes.
- In a saucepan, bring the butter, maple syrup, and brown sugar to a gentle boil. Stir in heavy cream. Add cider, ½ cup bourbon, and salt, and stir to combine. Cook for 15-20 minutes, stirring frequently to keep from sticking.
- Remove from heat and add the vanilla and the 2 tbsp. bourbon. Stir to combine.
- Pour sauce over baked bread pudding.

Bacon-Bourbon Pecan Pie

Who don't know that pecan pie ranks high on the list of traditional Southern desserts? How can y'all possibly improve it? I mean, it's pretty much pastry perfection. Well, leave it to me to add the twist *of bacon and bourbon and take perfection to a whole other level.*

Serves 6-8

INGREDIENTS:

6 strips bacon, diced
1½ cups pecans, whole or chopped
1 cup light corn syrup
½ cup white sugar
½ cup brown sugar
3 tbsp. butter, melted
3 eggs
2 tsp. vanilla
4 tbsp. bourbon
Pinch of salt
1 Tried-and-True Piecrust, unbaked (see index)

This is great served with bourbon ice cream or bourbon whipped cream.

DIRECTIONS:

· Preheat oven to 350 degrees.

· In a skillet over medium heat, cook bacon until crispy. Then add the pecans and stir for a few minutes until lightly toasted. Remove from heat and let cool.

· In a mixing bowl, stir the syrup and sugars until combined. Add the butter, eggs, vanilla, bourbon, and salt; stir to combine.

· Stir in the bacon-pecan mixture.

· Pour into piecrust. Place on a baking sheet and cover with foil.

· Bake for 35 minutes. Remove foil, and bake another 40-45 minutes or until there is still a slight jiggle in the middle.

· Remove pie and allow to cool to room temp.

Blueberry-Lemon Hand Pies

Hand pies originated as a means of convenience. Easy to pick up and take on the go, they were perfect for workers to grab after eatin' lunch or to pack in lunchboxes without muss or fuss. The most traditional "handheld" in the South is a fried apple pie, but y'all can put just about anything into one, from sweet to savory. My twist is to make this cute li'l pastry with the burst of sweet blueberries and the tartness of tangy lemon. But don't think y'all have to take just one of these. I mean, there's no law that says you can't use two hands.

Serves 16

INGREDIENTS:

2 cups fresh blueberries
¾ cup white sugar
½ tsp. ground ginger
Zest and juice of 1 lemon
½ tsp. vanilla
Pinch of salt
1 egg, beaten
16 frozen unbaked biscuits, thawed
Veggie oil for frying

GLAZE:

3 cups powdered sugar
1 tbsp. lemon juice
1 tbsp. milk
Zest of 1 lemon

These hand pies can be made with any berry.

DIRECTIONS:

- In a mixing bowl, stir the blueberries, sugar, ginger, lemon zest and juice, vanilla, and salt until combined, mashing slightly.

- On a floured surface, roll each biscuit into a 5-inch circle. Place 2 tbsp. blueberry mixture in the center of each dough circle. Using a pastry brush, moisten the edges with beaten egg. Bring dough over filling, forming a half-moon, and seal, crimping edge with a fork.

- Place filled pies on a parchment-lined baking sheet.

- Pour 3 inches oil into a Dutch oven, and bring to 350 degrees, as measured on a kitchen thermometer. Fry 2 pies in hot oil until golden brown. Transfer to a paper-towel-lined tray to drain.

- Repeat until all are fried.

- To make the glaze, whisk the powdered sugar, lemon juice, and milk together in a bowl.

- Dip the tops of each pie into the glaze.

- Transfer to a serving platter and garnish with lemon zest.

Bourbon-Cherry Mousse Jars

Cherries were not somethin' we had on the farm, but we were lucky enough to have folks bring us some ever' now and then. Of course, Granny was gonna whip 'em up in a sweet and tart cherry pie. As I got older, I preferred my cherries on cheesecake. One of my favorite twists on cheesecake is to put it in a jar, and of course, my favorite twist on ever'thing is bourbon. So, a double twist just seemed the right thing to do: cheesecake and bourbon in a jar.

Serves 8

PECAN-GRAHAM CRUST:
2 sleeves graham crackers, crushed
¼ cup minced pecans
¼ cup brown sugar
8 (8 oz.) mason jars or dessert cups

BOURBON CHERRIES:
3 tbsp. butter
3 cups frozen or fresh pitted black cherries
½ cup white sugar
⅓ cup bourbon

MOUSSE:
8 oz. cream cheese, room temp
1 cup sour cream
½ cup light brown sugar
1 tbsp. vanilla
3 cups heavy cream

GARNISH:
2 cups sweetened whipped cream
16 fresh cherries with stems
½ cup chocolate shavings
Sprigs of mint

> When working with heavy cream, never beat too long or it will turn to butter.

DIRECTIONS:

- To make the crust, combine the crushed graham crackers, pecans, and sugar in a small bowl, place 2 tbsp. crust mixture into the bottom of each jar or cup.

- To make the bourbon cherries, melt the butter in a large skillet over medium heat. Add cherries, sugar, and bourbon. Cook until cherries start to soften, about 8-10 minutes. Let cool.

- Divide the cherry mixture among the jars, over the crust layer.

- To make the mousse, place the cream cheese, sour cream, sugar, and vanilla in a stand-mixer bowl, and beat until smooth and creamy. Scrape down sides and add the heavy cream. Start mixer on low. When mixture starts to thicken, turn mixer to high, and beat for 2-3 minutes, or until stiff peaks form.

- Divide the mousse among the jars, over the cherry layer.

- Place a dollop of whipped cream on top, and garnish with cherries, chocolate shavings, and mint.

Easy Appalachian Stack Cake

This recipe is as near and dear to my heart as any recipe there is. One reason is because it is rooted in Appalachian tradition, and the other reason is because it was something special that my great-grandmother Maxey made at Christmastime. It wasn't made often, because it was a true labor of love, taking hours to prepare. I wanted to make it quicker and easier for folks to enjoy the wonderful flavors and memories of a good, old-fashioned stack cake, so I gave it the quick and easy twist of using prepared applesauce.

Serves 12-16

INGREDIENTS:
2 cups pancake mix
1 cup whole buttermilk
2 eggs
1 tsp. vanilla
2 tsp. apple pie spice

APPLE FILLING:
4 (15 oz.) cans applesauce
¼ cup butter, melted
1 cup dark brown sugar, packed
1 tbsp. ground cinnamon
¼ tsp. ground cloves

GARNISH:
Dried apple slices

This is one of those desserts where the longer it sets, the better it gets.

DIRECTIONS:
- In a bowl, whisk the pancake mix, buttermilk, eggs, vanilla, and pie spice until smooth. Let stand for 20 minutes.

- In a bowl, stir the apple filling ingredients until combined.

- Preheat a griddle or griddle pan to 350 degrees. Using a ¼ cup measure, pour enough batter to spread out into an 8-inch circle. Cook until brown, flip, and brown other side. Remove and place on a parchment-lined baking sheet. Continue frying cakes until all batter is gone.

- Once all the cakes are cooked, place 1 cake on a cake stand, and top cake with ¼ cup apple filling, until all cakes and filling are used.

- Garnish with dried apples.

Butterscotch-Apple Crisp

Y'all just can't beat a good fruit crisp. Whether you call it a cobbler or a buckle, I think we can all agree to call it delicious. I love butterscotch paired with apples, so it seemed natural to add a butterscotch twist to my traditional apple crisp recipe.

Serves 10

INGREDIENTS:
Nonstick cooking spray
3 cups diced yellow apples (about 3 apples)
1 small bag wrapped, hard butterscotch candy discs
$\frac{1}{2}$ cup water

CRISP TOPPING:
1 sleeve butter crackers, crushed
3 cups crushed vanilla wafers
$\frac{1}{2}$ cup quick-cook oats
1 cup butter, melted
2 tsp. vanilla

GARNISH:
2 cups vanilla whipped topping
$\frac{1}{2}$ cup crushed butterscotch candy

This can be made with
any type of apple or pear.

DIRECTIONS:

- Preheat oven to 350 degrees. Spray an 11x7 casserole dish with nonstick cooking spray.

- Spread apples in an even layer in the bottom of dish.

- Unwrap butterscotch discs and place in a saucepan over medium-low heat. Add the water. Cook, stirring often, until discs are melted. Remove from heat and pour over apples.

- To make the crisp topping, in a bowl, combine the crackers, vanilla wafers, and oats. Sprinkle over the top of the apple mixture. Mix the butter and vanilla, and drizzle over the top.

- Bake for 30-40 minutes or until toasty and bubbly.

- Spoon into serving dishes. Top each with whipped topping and a little crushed butterscotch.

Crunchy Peanut Butter Cookie Sammies

Nothin' beats a fresh, outta-the-oven peanut butter cookie . . . unless, of course, you give it a twist by takin' two peanut butter cookies, addin' a yummy marshmallow fluffin' between 'em, and slappin' 'em together in a sweet li'l cookie sandwich.

Makes 1 dozen

INGREDIENTS:
Nonstick cooking spray
1 cup packed dark brown sugar
1 cup white sugar
½ cup veggie shortening
½ cup butter
1 cup smooth peanut butter
½ tsp. salt
2 eggs
1 tbsp. vanilla
2 tsp. baking soda
2¼ cups all-purpose flour
1 cup chopped dry roasted peanuts
1 cup puffed rice cereal

This can be made with any nut butter.

FILLING:
2 cups marshmallow fluff
1 cup veggie shortening
⅓ cup smooth peanut butter
2 cups powdered sugar
1 tsp. vanilla

GARNISH:
1 cup crushed peanuts
¼ cup puffed rice cereal

DIRECTIONS:
- Preheat oven to 350 degrees. Line a baking sheet with parchment paper, and lightly spray with nonstick cooking spray.

- Using a stand mixer, cream sugars, shortening, butter, peanut butter, and salt until light and fluffy.

- Add the eggs and vanilla; mix until well combined.

- Mix baking soda and flour together and add to creamed mixture. Fold in the peanuts and cereal.

- Roll half the cookie dough into 12 walnut-size balls and place on prepared baking sheet. Do not mash down.

- Bake for 10-12 minutes. Transfer cookies to a cooling rack. Repeat with the rest of the dough.

- To make the filling, in a mixing bowl, mix fluff, shortening, and peanut butter until smooth and fluffy. Mix in the powdered sugar, and vanilla.

- When cookies are cool, turn 12 cookies upside down, place 3 tbsp. filling on each cookie, and top with remaining cookies, forming sandwiches. Mash down slightly.

- In a small bowl, mix the crushed peanuts and the rice cereal. Then roll the edges of the cookies in the mixture to cover the filling.

Must-Have Custard Pie with 7-Minute Meringue

Ever'one knew to ask Aunt Jean if they wanted a custard pie, because no one around could beat her. It didn't matter if it was chocolate, coconut, or lemon—Aunt Jean was the baker of choice. I've already told y'all about usin' my Award-Winnin' 7-Minute Frostin' recipe as a meringue. Well now's your chance to do that, with my meringue-toppin' twist on a simple custard pie.

Serves 8

INGREDIENTS:

¾ cup sugar
3 tbsp. cornstarch
3 egg yolks (use the whites in the frostin')
2 cups whole milk
1 tbsp. vanilla
1 (9 inch) baked piecrust
Award-Winnin' 7-Minute Frostin' (see index)

For chocolate custard pie, add 3 tbsp. cocoa powder when cooking the filling; for coconut, stir in 1 cup shredded sweetened coconut when custard is thick; and for lemon, add the zest of 1 lemon.

DIRECTIONS:

- In a saucepan, whisk sugar and cornstarch until combined. Whisk in the egg yolks and milk. Over medium heat, stir constantly.

- Let mixture come to a boil, and keep stirring until thick.

- Remove from stove and stir in vanilla.

- Pour into baked piecrust.

- After pie is cooled, top with frosting and swirl. Place under the broiler if you want a toasted meringue.

Granny Creech's Cushaw Pie

Now I know some of y'all know what a cushaw is, but for those of you who are shakin' your heads, I'm gonna give you a Cushaw 101 class. A cushaw is a green-and-white striped, crookneck squash—that's right, the one y'all think is only for decoratin' your fodder shock with. Sign up for Fodder Shock 101. Granny Creech always grew a lot of cushaws and punkin's, for makin' fall-time pies. I guess you could say that a cushaw pie is a twist *on its cousin, the punkin' pie.*

Serves 8

INGREDIENTS:
1 Tried-and-True Piecrust (see index)
2½ cups cooked and mashed cushaw
¼ cup evaporated milk
2 eggs, beaten
2 tsp. vanilla
1 cup white sugar
1 tbsp. all-purpose flour
¼ tsp. salt
½ tsp. ground nutmeg
2 tbsp. butter, melted

If you can't find cushaw, you can use butternut squash or acorn squash.

DIRECTIONS:

- Preheat oven to 450 degrees. Line a large baking sheet with foil.

- Place piecrust into a 9-inch, buttered pie pan; crimp edges of crust.

- In a mixing bowl, whisk cushaw, evaporated milk, eggs, and vanilla.

- Add sugar, flour, salt, nutmeg, and butter, and mix well.

- Pour into unbaked piecrust. Bake for 10 minutes. Reduce heat to 350 degrees, and bake another 40-45 minutes or until there is still a slight jiggle in the middle.

- Remove from oven and allow to cool before serving.

Hummingbird Tart

A hummingbird cake is an heirloom cake that has been passed down through many Southern generations. It's no wonder that one of the most esteemed county-fair blue ribbons a Southern baker can earn is for hummingbird cake. Now, it takes some guts to twist such a generational favorite, but I put on my big-boy whitey tighties on and did it. I made a deconstructed hummingbird cake fly straight into a tart shell, with all the tropical flavors that our ancestors intended.

Serves 8

INGREDIENTS:
Nonstick cooking spray
3 cups pretzels
1 cup dried banana chips
¼ cup packed brown sugar
½ tsp. ground cinnamon
6 tbsp. butter, melted

Make sure to drain the pineapple very well. It should be patted dry.

FILLING:
8 oz. cream cheese, room temp
2 tbsp. butter, room temp
1 small box French vanilla instant pudding
½ tsp. ground cinnamon
1 (20 oz.) can crushed pineapple, drained and patted dry
½ cup chopped pecans

GARNISH:
2 cups sweetened whipped cream
Dried banana chips
Dried pineapple slices
½ cup pecans, chopped

DIRECTIONS:
- Preheat oven to 350 degrees. Spray an 8-inch tart pan with nonstick cooking spray.
- In a food processor, pulse the pretzels, banana chips, brown sugar, and cinnamon until very fine. With the processor running, drizzle in the melted butter, until mixture looks like wet sand.
- Press pretzel mixture into the bottom and up the sides of the pan, making sure that the crust is even. Bake for 15-20 minutes. Remove from oven and let cool completely.
- To make the filling, using a stand mixer, whip the cream cheese, butter, pudding, and cinnamon until light and fluffy, about 4-5 minutes.
- Add the drained pineapple and pecans, and fold to combine.
- Spread the filling into the cooled crust.
- Cover and place in the fridge for at least 2 hours or overnight.
- When ready to serve, top with whipped cream, dried fruit, and pecans.

Kentucky Bourbon Cake with Chocolate Ganache

I'd like to think I was the first to come up with a Kentucky bourbon cake, but with a little research, anyone can see that it has been around for decades and probably longer. I mean, at some point, someone has had to realize that ever'thing is better with bourbon, includin' cake. The twist on two of my favorite things, cake and bourbon, is to add an awe-inspirin' chocolate ganache with bourbon to an already boozy confection.

Serves 12-14

INGREDIENTS:
Nonstick cooking spray
1 box yellow cake mix
1 small box French vanilla instant pudding
4 eggs
½ cup veggie oil
¼ cup water
¼ cup bourbon
1 cup chopped pecans

To check if a cake is done, insert a toothpick in the middle, and if it comes out clean, the cake is done.

SOAK:
½ cup butter
1 cup packed light brown sugar
¼ cup water
½ cup bourbon

BOURBON GANACHE:
10 oz. semisweet chocolate chips
½ cup heavy cream
3 tbsp. bourbon
2 tbsp. butter
½ tsp. vanilla

GARNISH:
Pecan halves

DIRECTIONS:
- Preheat oven to 350 degrees. Spray a 10-cup Bundt pan with nonstick cooking spray.

- In a mixing bowl, whisk the cake mix and pudding together. Add eggs, oil, water, and bourbon, and whisk until smooth. Fold in the pecans. Pour into prepared pan.

- Bake for 40-45 minutes or until golden brown.

- To make the soak, place the butter, sugar, water, and bourbon in a saucepan and bring to a boil. Let boil for 1 minute. Remove from heat and pour over the baked cake. Let it soak up the liquid for 10-15 minutes, then invert onto a serving plate.

- To make the bourbon ganache, place the chocolate chips in a heatproof bowl and set aside.

- In a small saucepan, add the cream and bourbon, and bring to a gentle bubble.

- Remove from heat and pour over chocolate chips. Let stand for 3-5 minutes, then stir until all chips are melted.

- Whisk in the butter and vanilla. Let stand for 15-20 minutes. Spoon over cake, and garnish with pecans.

New-South 'Nanner Puddin' Trifle

Traditional 'nanner puddin' is a Southern-dessert staple. Y'all won't see a church potluck or a family dinner without it. It seems to be a trend for folks to put their own twist on this much-adored Southern treat, and, of course, I'm nothin' if not trendy. My 'nanner puddin' twist is to give it a li'l tang with sour cream, add a sweet crunch with vanilla sandwich cookies, and layer all that traditional 'nanner puddin' goodness into a gorgeous trifle.

Serves 10

INGREDIENTS:
2 small boxes French vanilla or white chocolate instant pudding
3 cups whole milk
1 cup heavy cream
1 tbsp. vanilla
½ cup sour cream
1 family pack vanilla sandwich cookies, crushed, divided
4-6 ripe bananas, divided
1 tub extra-creamy whipped topping

Use traditional vanilla wafers if you don't have the cookies on hand.

DIRECTIONS:
- In a mixing bowl, whisk pudding, milk, cream, vanilla, and sour cream until thick.
- Measure 1 cup crushed cookies and reserve for garnish.
- Place half of the remaining crushed cookies in the bottom of a trifle bowl.
- Layer half of the pudding mix over the cookies.
- Slice half the bananas and layer evenly over the pudding.
- Add one more layer of cookies, and finish with the rest of the pudding and bananas.
- Place in the fridge for at least 2 hours.
- Remove from the fridge and spread the whipped topping evenly over the top.
- Garnish with reserved cookies.
- Cover and place in the fridge for at least 3 hours or overnight.

Orange-Slice Blondies

When I was growin' up, my favorite store-bought candy was orange slices. It makes me nostalgic just thinkin' about those sticky, sweet, orange-shaped wedges that was in Mom's covered glass candy dishes. I really wanted to pay homage to my favorite childhood candy by showcasin' it with a twist. *I chose a blondie to pair it with, because I thought it would really let the orange flavor shine, takin' me back to sneakin' orange slices from the candy bowl before supper.*

Serves 8

INGREDIENTS:
Nonstick cooking spray
1/2 cup butter, melted and cooled
1 cup light brown sugar
1 egg
1 tbsp. vanilla
1 cup self-rising flour
2 cups chopped orange-slice candy

CHEESECAKE SWIRL:
4 oz. cream cheese, room temp
1 tsp. vanilla
1 egg yolk
1/4 cup white sugar

GARNISH:
1/2 cup powdered sugar

This recipe can be made with your favorite gummy candy, such as peach rings.

DIRECTIONS:
- Preheat oven to 350 degrees. Spray an 8x8 baking dish with nonstick cooking spray.

- In a large mixing bowl, stir together butter and brown sugar. Add egg, vanilla, and flour.

- Fold the orange-slice candy into the blondie batter.

- In a bowl, mix the swirl ingredients until smooth and creamy.

- Spread half the blondie batter into the bottom of the prepared baking dish. Spread the cream cheese mixture over the batter. Spread the rest of the batter over the cream cheese layer.

- Using a knife or spoon, swirl all ingredients together.

- Bake for 35-40 minutes, or until golden brown.

- Remove dish and allow to cool completely. Cut into squares, and dust with powdered sugar.

Pistachio Ice-Cream Delight

My mom makes this recipe with coconut instead of pistachio. I wanted to keep this true to her tastes, so I gave it the twist *of substituting one of her favorite nuts. I love usin' vanilla ice cream as the milk component, because when it sets with the puddin' and half-and-half, it has a thick, velvety texture that's even better than ice cream.*

Serves 12

INGREDIENTS:
4 cups pretzels, crushed
1/2 cup butter, melted
Nonstick cooking spray
1 large or 2 small boxes pistachio instant pudding
1 1/2 cups half-and-half
2 tsp. vanilla
1/2 gal. vanilla ice cream, softened but not melted
8 oz. whipped topping, thawed

You can use any flavor pudding you like.

GARNISH:
1 cup chopped pistachios
1/2 cup crushed pretzels

DIRECTIONS:
- In a mixing bowl, stir crushed pretzels and melted butter until combined. Transfer to a 9x13 baking pan that has been sprayed with nonstick cooking spray, and press down.
- In a small bowl, whisk the pudding, half-and-half, and vanilla. Stir in softened ice cream.
- Spread over the top of pretzel layer.
- Top with thawed whipped topping and smooth out.
- Garnish with pistachios and crushed pretzels.
- Cover and place in the fridge for at least 2 hours or overnight.

Out-of-This-World Cake

This recipe was handed down to me by my aunt Brenda's mother-in-law. Even though we weren't related by blood, she treated me like one of her own grandchildren, and I called her Granny Aliene. The only twist I made to this cake was addin' some Southern pecans to the topping. I mean, when somethin' is out of this world, you don't mess with it.

Serves 12

INGREDIENTS:

4 cups graham cracker crumbs
2 cups white sugar
4 eggs, beaten
1 cup butter, melted
1 tsp. baking powder
1 cup whole milk
1 cup shredded sweetened coconut
1 cup chopped pecans
1 tsp. vanilla

Anytime you can't find pecans, just use walnuts.

TOPPING:

1 (20 oz.) can crushed pineapple
1 tbsp. all-purpose flour
1 cup white sugar
½ cup chopped pecans

GARNISH:

Maraschino cherries
Pecan halves

DIRECTIONS:

- Preheat oven to 350 degrees. Spray or butter a 9x13 baking pan.

- In a large mixing bowl, combine graham crackers, sugar, eggs, butter, baking powder, milk, coconut, pecans, and vanilla. Pour into prepared pan, and bake for 35-40 minutes.

- Remove from oven and let cool completely.

- In a medium saucepan, combine the topping ingredients. Bring to a boil, and let cook for 5 minutes. Remove from heat and let cool slightly. Pour over cake and smooth.

- Garnish with maraschino cherries and pecans.

Pap's Southern Blackberry Cake

This was the favorite cake of my dear, dear friend, Bill Bradford. Affectionately referred to as "Pap," Bill loved makin' and sharin' this cake with his family and friends. He used black walnuts from trees grown in his yard and Kentucky blackberries picked fresh from the briar. He would hoard his walnuts and frozen blackberries, so he could have his favorite cake all through the year. My twist on Pap's heritage recipe was to change his cream cheese icin' to a rich caramel frostin'.

Serves 12-14

INGREDIENTS:
Nonstick cooking spray
2 cups self-rising flour
2 tsp. ground cinnamon
1½ tsp. ground nutmeg
1 tsp. ground allspice
1 cup veggie oil
4 tbsp. butter, melted
1 cup white sugar
3 eggs
1 tsp. vanilla
2 cups blackberries

CARAMEL FROSTING:
½ cup butter
1 cup light brown sugar
¼ cup milk
5-6 cups powdered sugar
1 tsp. vanilla

GARNISH:
1 cup fresh blackberries
1 cup whole, toasted walnuts

When baking with fresh berries, make sure the cake pans are sprayed heavily, to ensure that the cakes do not stick.

DIRECTIONS:
- Preheat oven to 350 degrees. Spray three 8-inch round cake pans with nonstick cooking spray. Place a round piece of parchment in the bottom of each pan, and spray again.

- In a small mixing bowl, sift the first 4 ingredients.

- In a medium bowl, whisk the oil, butter, and sugar. Add the eggs and vanilla, and stir to combine.

- Add the flour mixture into the egg mixture, and stir until combined.

- Gently fold in the blackberries.

- Divide batter evenly among the prepared pans. Bake for 30-35 minutes or until a toothpick inserted in the middle comes out clean.

- Cool in pans for 5 minutes, then turn out onto cooling racks and allow to cool completely.

- To make the frosting, place the butter and brown sugar in a medium saucepan. Bring to a boil, and cook for 2 minutes.

- Remove from heat and carefully stir in the milk. Add powdered sugar and vanilla, stirring until thick enough to pour and spread.

- Assemble cake by placing 1 cake on a cake stand and frosting with ⅓ of the frosting. Add second cake, and continue until all the cakes and frosting have been used.

- Garnish with fresh blackberries and whole, toasted walnuts.

Scrumptious Sweet-Tater Bars

Sometimes I think I was born with a sweet tater in each hand. I love this sweet orange tuber any and ever' way it can be fixed. I've takin' one of the South's most iconic desserts, sweet-tater pie, and given it a twist by turnin' it into magic bars. Now, a magic cake or bar is a dessert that forms three layers when it bakes: a crust, a creamy center, and a tender top. Trust me, y'all will know why it's called "magic" as soon as you take the first bite.

Serves 12

This can be made ahead of time and frozen. Allow to thaw before serving.

INGREDIENTS:
Nonstick cooking spray
1½ cups white sugar
½ cup light brown sugar
1 cup self-rising flour
1 tsp. ground cinnamon
½ tsp. ground ginger
¼ tsp. ground cloves
1 cup milk
¾ cup butter, melted
2 tbsp. bourbon
4 eggs
2 tsp. vanilla
4 cups peeled and grated sweet taters

GARNISH:
2 cups whipped cream
1 cup chopped toasted pecans
1 tsp. ground nutmeg

DIRECTIONS:

- Preheat oven to 350 degrees. Spray a 9x13 baking pan with nonstick cooking spray.

- In a mixing bowl, stir sugars, flour, and spices until combined.

- Add the milk, butter, bourbon, eggs, and vanilla; stir to combine.

- Fold in the grated sweet taters.

- Pour into prepared pan. Bake for 40-45 minutes.

- When cooled, cut into squares. Garnish with whipped cream and pecans, and sprinkle with nutmeg.

Snowdrop Cookies

My dad's favorite cookie is a pecan shortbread dusted in powdered sugar; y'all may know 'em as Mexican weddin' cookies. We always called 'em snowdrop cookies, because we had 'em at Christmastime, and they looked like they had snow on 'em. I gave the traditional recipe a fruitcake-inspired twist by addin' orange zest and dried fruit.

Makes 2 dozen

INGREDIENTS:

2 cups self-rising flour
¼ cup brown sugar, packed
¼ cup white sugar
1 tsp. ground ginger
½ tsp. ground nutmeg
2 tbsp. orange zest
1 cup butter, cold, cut into cubes
1 egg, room temp
2 tsp. vanilla
⅛ cup candied ginger, minced
¾ cup dried currants
½ cup pecans, chopped
2 cups powdered sugar, for rolling

You can make these cookies 2-3 months in advance and freeze.

DIRECTIONS:

· Preheat oven to 350 degrees.

· In a stand-mixer bowl, place the flour, sugars, spices, and zest. Turn mixer to low, and mix for 20 seconds.

· Add the butter and mix until it resembles coarse cornmeal.

· Add egg and vanilla, and mix.

· Fold in ginger, currants, and nuts.

· Using a 1-oz. cookie scoop, place 12 dough balls on a lined baking sheet. Bake for 18 minutes.

· Remove and let cool for 5-8 minutes.

· Repeat with the rest of the dough.

· Roll cooled cookies in powdered sugar.

Tried-and-True Piecrust

Piecrust is one of those things that can stump even the best bakers. Most piecrusts are made with either cold milk or water. Granny Creech opted for milk, and she never had a piecrust fail. I learned a li'l twist from an old lady that I worked with years ago, and I have to say I was shocked to learn this secret from a tee-totaling church woman. But she swore she never snuck a sip. Her secret was ice-cold vodka. At the time, I didn't know how it worked—I just knew she baked the flakiest crusts I'd ever seen. I later learned it's all about the science of baking. Vodka provides the liquid required for the piecrust but limits the water content that triggers gluten development. That will be the only science lesson y'all will ever get from me.

Makes 2 pie sheets

INGREDIENTS:

3 cups all-purpose flour
1 tsp. salt
1 cup butter, cold, cut into small pieces
1/3 cup shortening
5-6 tbsp. vodka, ice cold

> When working with dough, always use a light hand or you will activate the gluten, causing the dough to be tough.

DIRECTIONS:

- In a large mixing bowl, sift flour and salt together.

- In a food processor, pulse flour mixture, butter, and shortening until it resembles coarse cornmeal.

- Add 1 tbsp. vodka at a time to flour mixture, pulsing between each addition, until dough forms a ball. This may not take all the vodka.

- Turn dough out onto a piece of plastic wrap. Using a very light hand, mold the dough into a 1-inch-thick disc. Wrap in the plastic wrap, and place in the fridge for 15-20 minutes. Make sure to always let your pie dough rest in the fridge until ready to use.

- Remove dough from fridge and cut in half. Wrap unused half and place back in fridge.

- Sprinkle work surface with flour.

- Roll dough into a round about ½-inch thick. Fold over into a half-moon, then fold once more to look like a pizza slice. Repeat this process 3-4 more times.

- After last roll, place in desired pie tin, cut off excess dough, and crimp edges. Place in freezer for 10 minutes.

- Repeat the fold-and-roll process with second disc of dough.

- Either fill and bake, or blind bake for cream pies.

Southern Coconut Layered Sheet Cake

Anyone from the South can identify with a traditional Texas sheet cake. Well, Lord knows, if one layer of cake is good, then six are even better. That's just one twist I've given a traditional sheet cake. The other twist is the fresh and light flavor of coconut, and children, I mean a lot of coconut. I promise, this lush, layered cake slathered with coconut frostin' will have y'all leapin' like lizards in a hailstorm.

Serves 8-10

INGREDIENTS:

Nonstick cooking spray
4 eggs, separated
¼ tsp. cream of tartar
Pinch of salt
1 tsp. vanilla
1 tsp. coconut extract
½ cup olive oil
½ cup water
½ cup coconut milk
1 box yellow cake mix
1 cup shredded coconut

FROSTING:

5 cups powdered sugar
5-6 tbsp. coconut milk
1 tsp. vanilla
2 tbsp. butter, melted
2 tbsp. coconut rum

GARNISH:

2 cups coconut

> When toasting coconut, watch closely to prevent burning.

DIRECTIONS:

- Preheat oven to 350 degrees. Line 2 rimmed baking sheets with parchment paper and lightly spray with nonstick cooking spray.

- In a stand-mixer bowl, place the egg whites, cream of tartar, and salt. Beat until stiff peaks form, and transfer to another bowl.

- In same mixer bowl, place the egg yolks, vanilla, coconut extract, oil, water, and coconut milk. Using the paddle attachment, mix well.

- Stir in the cake mix. Fold in coconut.

- Fold in half the egg whites, then fold in the rest of egg whites. Make sure to use a light hand, so the egg whites do not deflate.

- Divide the batter evenly between prepared pans, and smooth out. Bake for 20-25 minutes or until a toothpick inserted in the middle comes out clean.

- Remove and let cool for 3-5 minutes. Keep oven on.

- Cut each sheet cake into 3 equal parts.

- In a mixing bowl, mix all the frosting ingredients well. Reserve ½ cup frosting for the sides of the cake. Divide the rest of the frosting into 6 portions for the layers.
- Place coconut on a baking sheet and toast in oven for 3-5 minutes or until golden brown.
- Place 1 layer of cake on a serving platter. Ice with 1 portion frosting. Repeat with the rest of the layers, then ice the sides. Decorate all over with toasted coconut.

To-Die-For Chocolate-Mayo Cupcakes

A mayo cake is a depression-era cake, using mayo in place of eggs and oil. This recipe has been passed down through generations ever since, makin' it a heritage recipe that allowed folks to enjoy a good chocolate cake durin' hard times. It was obviously a recipe that worked, because it's still around today. A traditional mayo cake has a chocolate icin', so I decided to give it a twist by makin' cupcakes and slatherin' 'em with a homemade coconut-pecan frostin'.

Serves 12

INGREDIENTS:

4 cups self-rising flour
$3/4$ cup white sugar
$1/4$ cup dark brown sugar
$2/3$ cup cocoa powder
2 cups real mayo
1 tbsp. vanilla
2 cups + 2 tbsp. water
1 cup dark chocolate chips

FROSTING:

1 cup canned evaporated milk
1 cup sugar
3 egg yolks
$1/2$ cup butter
1 tsp. vanilla
$2^{2}/_{3}$ cups coconut
1 cup chopped pecans

Sometimes this batter makes a few more than 12 cupcakes. Just keep baking batches until all batter has been used.

DIRECTIONS:

- Preheat oven to 350 degrees. Line a 12-hole cupcake pan with liners.

- In large mixing bowl, whisk flour, sugars, and cocoa powder.

- In a small mixing bowl, whisk mayo, vanilla, and water. Add to flour mixture and whisk together until smooth.

- Fold in the chocolate chips.

- Fill each cupcake liner $2/3$ full.

- Bake for 20-25 minutes or until a toothpick inserted in the middle comes out clean. Remove from pan, place on a cooling rack, and allow to cool completely.

- To make the frosting, in a saucepan, whisk the first 5 ingredients. Cook over low heat, stirring, until thickened. Remove from heat, and fold in coconut and nuts.

- Let frosting cool to room temperature before frosting cupcakes.

True-South Sweet Tea Bundt Cake

Bundt cakes are nothin' new, but they have had a resurgence in the last few years. When I was young, I thought they were the fanciest-lookin' things ever. No Southern-inspired cookbook would be complete without a good Bundt-cake recipe, and as my very good friend Lisa reminded me, it would not be complete without some mention of sweet tea, which just happens to be our favorite drink of the nonalcoholic variety. Cheers to enjoyin' my sweet tea twist on traditional Bundt cake.

Serves 12

INGREDIENTS:
Nonstick cooking spray
1 box yellow cake mix
1 small box vanilla instant pudding
3/4 cup strong brewed tea
4 eggs, room temp
3/4 cup corn or canola oil
1 cup chopped pecans

GLAZE:
2 1/2 cups powdered sugar
1/3 cup butter, melted
1 tbsp. strong brewed tea

GARNISH:
1/2 cup chopped pecans
Sliced lemons

Substituting strong brewed coffee for the tea makes this a great coffee Bundt.

DIRECTIONS:
- Preheat oven to 350 degrees. Spray a 10-cup Bundt pan with nonstick cooking spray.

- In a large mixing bowl, mix cake mix, pudding, tea, eggs, and oil until combined. Fold in pecans.

- Pour batter into prepared pan. Bake for 45-50 minutes or until a toothpick inserted in the middle comes out clean.

- Remove from oven, and let cool in pan for about 20 minutes. Invert onto a serving plate.

- In a small bowl, whisk the glaze ingredients. Drizzle over cooled cake.

- Garnish with pecans and lemon slices.

Chapter 6

PICKLIN' AND PRESERVIN' (CONDIMENTS)

24-Hour Pickled Beets

Bacon 'Mater Jam

Balsamic Grape Jelly

Bourbon Pear Preserves

Citrus Spread

Bourbon-Onion Marmalade

Brined Cucumbers

Ever'day Bread and Butter Pickles

Cherry Orange Preserves

Easy Blueberry Jam

Fast-Pickled Okra

Icebox Blackberry Spread

Green 'Mater Chow-Chow

Kicked-Up Kiwi

'Mater-Berry Freezer Jam

No-Cook Strawberry Freezer Jam

Peach-Honey and Basil Preserves

Perfectly Pickled Pineapple

Pickled Mixed Veggies

Pickled Pearls and Corn

Quick-Pickled Radishes

Cannin' food to preserve it for future use has been around since the time of Napoleon. If you can eat it, you can pickle it or preserve it, whether it's a quick-pickled veggie to add to a meal or a sealed preserve meant to last throughout the year. It's such a treat to go to the pantry and pull out a jar of homemade jam or pickled veggies, long after the growin' season has ended.

When I was growin', up, it took my whole family all season long to can, preparin' for the winter months ahead. We canned ever'thing from green beans to blackberries, squash, and, believe it or not, even sausage.

Don't be intimidated by picklin' and preservin'—it's easier than you think. To get y'all started, I have some simple *twisted* recipes with some of your favorite fruits and veggies. Stick with me like a *hair in a biscuit*, and I'll have y'all picklin' and preservin' like a pro.

24-Hour Pickled Beets

Makes 1 quart

INGREDIENTS:
1 quart or 2 pint jars
2 (15 oz.) cans sliced beets in water, drained
1 cup white vinegar
1/3 cup apple cider vinegar
1 cup water
1 cup honey
1 tsp. salt
1 tsp. whole black peppercorns

Make sure the brine completely covers the beets in the jar.

DIRECTIONS:
- Place beets in jar.
- In a saucepan, over medium heat, bring vinegars, water, honey, salt, and peppercorns to a boil. Cook for 5 minutes.
- Pour brine over beets and tighten lid on the jar. Leave on counter for 24 hours, then place in fridge.

Bacon 'Mater Jam

Makes 1 quart

INGREDIENTS:
1 1/2 lb. tomatoes, cored, can be peeled
1 lb. bacon, cubed and cooked, reserve drippings
1 medium onion, diced
1/4 cup brown sugar
1/4 cup honey
2 tsp. paprika
1/2 tsp. crushed red pepper flakes
Salt and ground black pepper to taste
1 tbsp. vinegar
3 tbsp. bourbon

This recipe can be adjusted to make a bigger batch.

DIRECTIONS:
- Dice tomatoes fine.
- Place bacon drippings in a large saucepan and heat over medium heat. Add onions and cook until soft.
- Add sugar, honey, paprika, red pepper flakes, salt, and pepper. Stir to combine. Add the tomatoes and cook for 25-30 minutes, stirring often.
- Add the vinegar and bourbon, and cook until thick.
- Once it has a jam-like consistency, stir in the bacon.
- Place in a container with lid in fridge overnight.

Balsamic Grape Jelly

Makes 4 pints

INGREDIENTS:

4 pint jars
3 lb. black or purple seedless grapes
2 cups white sugar
1 tsp. lemon juice
3 tbsp. balsamic vinegar
¼ tsp. salt
½ tsp. ground black pepper

You can use any type or color of grape, as long as it is seedless.

DIRECTIONS:

- In a large pot, stir together the grapes, sugar, and lemon juice. Bring to a boil over medium heat, and cook for 20 minutes or until grapes start to burst open.

- Add vinegar, salt, and pepper. Return to a boil. Reduce heat to low, and cook for 30 minutes, or until thick.

- Place in jars and cover with lids. Leave on counter until cooled, then place in fridge.

Bourbon Pear Preserves

Makes 4 pints

INGREDIENTS:

4 pint jars
2 lb. pears, peeled and cored
3 tbsp. pectin powder
1 tsp. ground cinnamon
2 tbsp. lemon juice
¼ cup bourbon
3 cups white sugar

This can be made with peaches or apples.

DIRECTIONS:

- Rough chop pears. Transfer to a large Dutch oven, and mash with a potato masher until pears are mushy.

- Stir in the pectin, cinnamon, lemon juice, and bourbon. Bring mixture to a boil over medium heat.

- Add sugar, stirring to dissolve. Return to a boil, and cook for 2 minutes.

- Remove from heat. Ladle preserves into jars and cover with lids. Let cool on counter overnight, then place in fridge for 1-2 months.

Citrus Spread

Makes 2 cups

INGREDIENTS:

3 eggs
¾ cup white sugar
Pinch of salt
½ cup lemon juice
Zest of 1 lemon
Zest of 2 limes
Zest of ½ grapefruit
3 tbsp. butter

When zesting citrus, remember not to zest too deep or you will get the bitter pith.

DIRECTIONS:

- In a saucepan, whisk eggs, sugar, salt, juice, and all citrus zest together.

- Cook over low heat, stirring constantly. Mixture will start to thicken after 4-5 minutes. Keep stirring until very thick.

- Remove from heat and stir in the butter.

- Place in airtight container, and keep in fridge until ready to use.

Bourbon-Onion Marmalade

Makes 1 quart

INGREDIENTS:
½ cup extra-virgin olive oil
2 tbsp. bacon drippings
½ cup butter
4 lb. onions, thinly sliced
1 tbsp. honey
Salt and ground black pepper to taste
1 cup low-sodium chicken stock
4 tbsp. balsamic vinegar
1 cup bourbon

Water or more stock can be substituted for the bourbon.

DIRECTIONS:
- In a large Dutch oven, heat olive oil, bacon drippings, and butter over medium heat.

- Add onions, honey, salt, and pepper. Sauté until onions are tender.

- Add stock and balsamic vinegar, and cook for 15-20 minutes.

- Reduce heat to low. Stir in the bourbon and cook for 30 minutes, or until it becomes semi-thick.

Brined Cucumbers

Makes 1 quart

INGREDIENTS:
1 quart jar
2 large cucumbers, peeled and sliced
1 medium onion, sliced
1 orange or red bell pepper, cored and sliced
1 tbsp. coarse salt
Water to cover

This will keep in the fridge for one week.

DIRECTIONS:
- Place cucumbers, onions, and peppers in jar.

- Add salt, and cover with water.

- Cover with lid and place in fridge for 4 hours or overnight.

Ever'day Bread and Butter Pickles

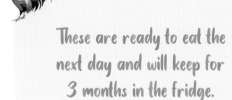

Makes 2 quarts

INGREDIENTS:

2 quart jars
8 large cucumbers, peeled and sliced
1½ tbsp. kosher salt
1 medium onion, sliced
2 jars pimentos, drained

BRINE:

1 cup white sugar
½ cup packed light brown sugar
1 cup white vinegar
½ cup apple cider vinegar
3 tbsp. whole mustard seed
½ tsp. dill seed
½ tsp. turmeric

These are ready to eat the
next day and will keep for
3 months in the fridge.

DIRECTIONS:

- Place sliced cucumbers in a bowl and cover with the salt. Toss to coat. Let stand for 1 hour.

- Place the cucumbers in a colander and rinse the salt off. Return cucumbers to bowl. Add the onions and pimentos, and toss.

- In a saucepan, stir together the brine ingredients until sugars have dissolved. Bring to a boil. Pour over cucumbers, and let stand for 2 hours.

- After cucumber mix has stood, place into jars and cover with brine. Tighten lids on the jars, and place in fridge overnight.

Cherry Orange Preserves

Makes 2 quarts

INGREDIENTS:

2 quart jars
32 oz. frozen dark sweet, pitted cherries, thawed
Zest of 2 medium oranges
1 cup white sugar
$\frac{1}{2}$ tsp. almond extract
6-8 sprigs thyme, minced
3 tbsp. cornstarch
$\frac{1}{4}$ cup orange juice

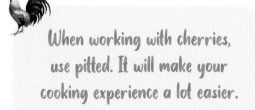

When working with cherries, use pitted. It will make your cooking experience a lot easier.

DIRECTIONS:

- In a large Dutch oven, stir the cherries, zest, and sugar until combined.

- Cook over medium-high heat for 20-25 minutes, stirring often.

- Reduce heat to low. Stir in almond extract and thyme. Continue cooking for 10 minutes.

- In a small bowl, whisk the cornstarch and orange juice together.

- Pour cornstarch mixture into cherries; stir until thickened.

- Once thick, ladle hot preserves into jars. Let cool on counter, tighten lids on the jars, and place in fridge.

Easy Blueberry Jam

Makes 1 pint

INGREDIENTS:
1 pint jar
2 cups fresh blueberries, washed
¾ cup white sugar
¼ cup honey
1 tsp. lime juice

This recipe can be used with any berry.

DIRECTIONS:

- In a medium saucepan, stir together the berries, sugar, honey, and lime juice.

- Cook over medium-low heat, stirring, until sugar has dissolved. Cook for 10-15 minutes. Reduce heat to low and continue cooking for about 20-25 minutes. Stir often to make sure it does not stick.

- Once berries are tender, it will look like syrup but will thicken up once cooled.

- Ladle hot jam into jar. Let cool on counter, tighten lid on the jar, and place in fridge.

Fast-Pickled Okra

Makes 2 pints

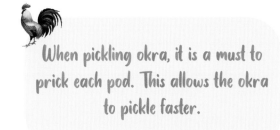

When pickling okra, it is a must to prick each pod. This allows the okra to pickle faster.

INGREDIENTS:
2 pint jars
2 cloves garlic
1 lb. whole fresh okra
6-8 sprigs dill
2 tsp. dill seeds
2 cups white vinegar
¼ cup water
1 tbsp. kosher salt
1 tsp. white sugar
½ tsp. crushed red pepper flakes

DIRECTIONS:
- Place 1 clove garlic in each jar.
- Wash and dry the okra. Prick each pod with the tip of a knife. Add okra to jars, fitting them in tightly by alternating stem ends up and down.
- Divide the dill and place in each jar.
- In a saucepan, bring dill seeds, vinegar, water, salt, sugar, and red pepper flakes to a boil.
- Pour brine over okra, making sure the liquid comes above okra but leaving ½ inch of space at the top.
- Leave on counter until cooled, tighten lids on the jars, and place in fridge for 3-5 days before eating.
- These will keep for 2 months in the fridge.

Icebox Blackberry Spread

Makes 1 pint

When mashing berries, you can also place in a zip-top bag and crush.

INGREDIENTS:
2 cups fresh or frozen blackberries
1 cup white sugar
⅓ cup Sure-Jell fruit pectin
1 tsp. ground ginger
1 tbsp. lime or lemon juice

DIRECTIONS:
- In a large bowl, mash berries with a potato masher or back of a large spoon, until no large chunks remain.
- Add the sugar, Sure-Jell, ginger, and juice. Stir for 3 minutes.
- Let stand for 8 minutes, then place in a jar or airtight container.
- Keep in fridge until ready to use.

Green 'Mater Chow-Chow

Makes 2 quarts

INGREDIENTS:

2 quart jars
4 medium green tomatoes, cored and chopped
½ onion, chopped
1 green bell pepper, chopped
1 jalapeno, seeded and chopped
½ cup white vinegar
1 tbsp. coarse salt
1 tbsp. white sugar
1 tsp. whole mustard seed

You should always wear kitchen gloves when working with hot peppers.

DIRECTIONS:

- In a large saucepan, place green tomatoes, onion, bell pepper, and jalapeno.
- Wearing kitchen gloves, mix and squish with hands.
- Add the vinegar, salt, sugar, and mustard seeds. Mix with hands for 2-3 minutes.
- Add to jars, packing tightly. Tighten lids on the jars, set jars in a shallow pan, and leave on counter for 3-4 days. Then place in fridge.

Kicked-Up Kiwi

Makes 2 pints

INGREDIENTS:

2 pint jars
10-12 kiwifruit
4 sprigs rosemary
2 cups water
¾ cup white sugar
1 tsp. whole black peppercorns
¼ cup vodka

When peeling kiwi, cut the ends off and then use a spoon to peel.

DIRECTIONS:

- Peel and quarter the kiwifruit, and place in jars.
- Divide the rosemary between jars.
- In a small saucepan, bring the water, sugar, and peppercorns to a simmer. Remove from heat and stir in vodka. Pour over fruit.
- Tighten lids on jars. Leave on counter for 2 hours, then place in fridge overnight.

'Mater-Berry Freezer Jam

Makes 6 pints

INGREDIENTS:
4 cups peeled, chopped red tomatoes
4 cups white sugar
2 tsp. lemon juice
1 (6 oz.) box raspberry or strawberry gelatin

This recipe is very easy to double.

DIRECTIONS:
- In a large Dutch oven, mash tomatoes with a potato masher.
- Add sugar and lemon juice. Cook for 20 minutes, stirring often.
- Remove from heat and let stand for 5 minutes.
- Stir in gelatin, and mix well.
- Pour into jars or airtight freezer containers. Leave on counter until cooled, then store in freezer.

No-Cook Strawberry Freezer Jam

Makes 6 cups

INGREDIENTS:
6 half-pint jars
2 cups crushed strawberries (about 1 quart berries)
4 cups white sugar
¾ cup water
1 box Sure-Jell fruit pectin

This can be made with any berry.

DIRECTIONS:
- In a mixing bowl, thoroughly mix the strawberries and sugar. Let stand for 10 minutes.
- In a small saucepan, boil water and Sure-Jell for 1 minute, stirring constantly.
- Remove from heat and stir into fruit. Continue stirring for 3 minutes.
- Ladle jam quickly into jars, cover at once with lids, and tighten.
- Let stand on counter overnight, then store in freezer.

Peach-Honey and Basil Preserves

Makes 4 cups

INGREDIENTS:

1 lb. fresh peaches, peeled and sliced
½ cup white sugar
3 tbsp. honey
1 tbsp. lemon juice
10 fresh basil leaves, thinly sliced (julienned)

An easy way to test if preserves, jams, and jellies are cooked thick enough is to set a saucer in the freezer and then place a drop or two of the mixture on the frozen plate. If it sets up, it's ready. If it remains thin, keep cooking.

DIRECTIONS:

- In a large Dutch oven, over medium heat, bring peaches, sugar, honey, and lemon juice to a boil, stirring often.

- Cook until thick, about 12-15 minutes. If not thick, keep cooking and stirring until it thickens.

- Remove from heat and stir in sliced basil.

- Ladle preserves into jars or heat-proof containers. Let cool completely before tightening lids on the containers, then store in fridge.

Perfectly Pickled Pineapple

Makes 1 quart

INGREDIENTS:
$\frac{1}{2}$ tsp. salt
$\frac{1}{3}$ cup powdered sugar
$\frac{3}{4}$ cup water
$\frac{2}{3}$ cup white vinegar
1 tbsp. whole black peppercorns
1 pineapple, peeled, cored, and cut into spears
1 small jalapeno, sliced

> For less heat, take the seeds out of the jalapeno.

DIRECTIONS:
- In a saucepan, over medium heat, bring salt, powdered sugar, water, vinegar, and peppercorns to a boil. Cook for 5 minutes.
- Add the pineapple and jalapeno, and cook another 5 minutes.
- Remove from heat and let cool to room temp.
- Place in a jar or container with lid in fridge for 12 hours before eating.

Pickled Mixed Veggies

Makes 2 quarts

INGREDIENTS:
2 quart jars
5-6 cups sliced or cubed mixed veggies, such as beets, carrots, green beans, cauliflower, bell peppers, summer squash
4 cloves garlic, sliced
1 tbsp. whole fennel seed
2 tsp. whole mustard seed
3-4 sprigs dill

> When preparing the veggies, try to cut them all to the same size. That way they will pickle at the same rate.

BRINE:
2 cups white vinegar
2 cups water
2 tbsp. kosher salt
4 tbsp. white sugar

DIRECTIONS:
- Place prepared veggies and the garlic in jars. Sprinkle in the spices and dill.
- In a saucepan, bring the brine ingredients to a hard boil.
- Pour brine over veggies. Press veggies down with back of a spoon to ensure a tight fit.
- Tighten lids on the jars. Leave on counter for 2 hours, then place in fridge overnight.

Pickled Pearls and Corn

Makes 2 quarts

INGREDIENTS:

2 quart jars
3 cups frozen pearl onions, thawed
2 cups white or yellow frozen corn, thawed
2 cloves garlic
$3/4$ cup white vinegar
$1/2$ cup water
$1/3$ cup white sugar
$1/3$ cup olive oil
2 tsp. all-purpose steak seasoning
2 tsp. salt

For extra spice, add a serrano pepper cut in half to each jar.

DIRECTIONS:

- In a large bowl, toss the onions and corn to combine,

- Place 1 clove garlic in bottom of each jar. Fill jars with onions and corn,

- In same bowl, whisk the vinegar, water, sugar, oil, steak seasoning, and salt together until sugar has dissolved. Pour over veggies in jars.

- Tighten lids on the jars, then place in fridge overnight.

Quick-Pickled Radishes

Makes 1 quart

INGREDIENTS:
1 quart jar
2 bunches radishes, washed and sliced
1 small purple onion, sliced
1-inch piece ginger, peeled and sliced

BRINE:
$1\frac{1}{2}$ cups white vinegar
1 cup honey
$\frac{1}{2}$ cup water
1 tsp. whole mustard seed
1 tsp. celery seed
2 tsp. whole black peppercorns
2 tsp. kosher salt

When peeling ginger, use a spoon. It is easier and safer than a knife.

DIRECTIONS:
- Place radishes, onion, and ginger in jar.
- In a saucepan, over medium heat, bring the brine ingredients to a boil. Cook for 3 minutes. Pour brine over radishes.
- Tighten lid on the jar, then place in fridge for 2 or more hours.

A Li'l Extra
(Equivalents/Conversions)

Oven Temp Equivalents

250°F = 120°C	400°F = 200°C
275°F = 135°C	425°F = 220°C
300°F = 150°C	450°F = 230°C
325°F = 160°C	475°F = 240°C
350°F = 180°C	500°F = 260°C
375°F = 190°C	

Measurement Conversions

CUP	FLUID OZ	TBSP	TSP	MILLILITER
1 C	8 OZ	16 TBSP	48 TSP	237 ML
3/4 C	6 OZ	12 TBSP	36 TSP	177 ML
2/3 C	5 OZ	11 TBSP	32 TSP	158 ML
1/2 C	4 OZ	8 TBSP	24 TSP	118 ML
1/3 C	3 OZ	5 TBSP	16 TSP	79 ML
1/4 C	2 OZ	4 TBSP	12 TSP	59 ML
1/8 C	1 OZ	2 TBSP	6 TSP	30 ML
1/16 C	.5 OZ	1 TBSP	3 TSP	15 ML

A Li'l Extra

FAMILY PHOTO ALBUM

My mom, Connie, and me

My uncle Danny and me

Granny Creech and me

Great-Granny Moren and me

Papaw Creech and me

Me eatin' fresh pears

Aunt Mae and me

Jim and Nannie Phipps Creech

The Creech Family
Glenna Mae Creech

Connie Lynn Creech

Papaw and Granny Creech

Imogene Creech

Brenda Madge Creech

Great-Grandfather and Grandmother
Johnnie Creech and Dora North Creech

Great-Granddaddy and Grandmother
Marion Franklin Phipps and Sallie Dugger Phipps

Mom and Sue Sue

Papaw Creech and
Uncle Walkie

Uncle Walkie, Uncle Jim,
and Uncle Bob

Sue Sue, Aunt Mae,
and Aunt Brenda

Clockwise from bottom:

Uncle Walkie, Uncle Danny, Aunt Jean, Dad, Aunt Brenda, Aunt Irene, Uncle Morris

Me on Aunt Brenda's lap

Me holding a fish

Family on the Farm
Aunt Jean and Great-Granddaddy Phipps

Granny Creech's home
where she was raised

Farm life in Leslie, Laurel, and
Taylor counties, Kentucky
1940s to 1960s

Granny Aliene Viars

My mom, Connie Lynn Creech Smith
Cousin Susan George Weaver
Granny Creech
Great Papaw and Great-Granny Phipps
(bottom right)

Aunt Brenda and Mom at Old Home Place

Connie Lynn Creech Smith
1964

Great-Great-Grandmother
Alice Sutton Maxey

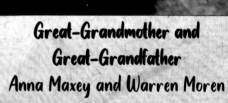

Great-Grandmother and
Great-Grandfather
Anna Maxey and Warren Moren

Great-Aunt Louise Moren
standing in front of the
family store

Great-Grandparents
Jim and Lena Smith
(center and right)

Great-Uncles and -Aunts
Harry Smith (top left)
J. D. Smith (top right)
Edith Smith (center left)
George Smith (front left)
Jenny Smith (smallest child)
Eugene Smith
Wandella Smith

Papaw George and Granny
Jean Moren Smith

THANK-YOU NOTES

Being raised by true Southern ladies and gentlemen, I was always taught to send thank-you notes as an expression of my gratitude for a gift or act of kindness. Lord knows, I couldn't have accomplished what I have without the graciousness of so many special people throughout the years—from ancestors I've never met, passing down time-honored recipes; to greatly loved and treasured family members who have passed on; to family and friends who are still here, inspiring me and pushing me every day. There are so many such folks that it would literally take an eternity to write everyone a thank-you note. I must, however, acknowledge a few important people who I feel have been so instrumental in bringing me to the point of realizing the lifelong dream of sharing heritage food and recipes with y'all.

I must start out with the reason I am even in this world, my mom and dad, Connie and Bill Smith, who have always shown me endless love and support in all things I have done. They raised me in a loving, kind home where family was the most important thing. Thank you, Mom and Dad, for all you have done for me and the examples you have set that have helped guide me.

If you have read the cookbook, you know how important my extended family has been in teaching me an appreciation for hard work and a love for Southern-country cooking. Those who I have loved dearly and who have passed on include: Papaw and Granny Creech, Aunt Jean, Aunt Mae, Papaw George and Granny Jean, Great-Granny Moren, Granny Aliene, and Pap Bradford. All of these beautiful souls are with me every day, from my country slang to the love I put into every dish.

Aunt Brenda and Uncle Danny, who are like my second set of parents, have always been my pep section through all of my crazy undertakings. Thank you, Aunt Brenda, for loving me and teaching me such wonderful recipes. Thank you, Uncle Danny, for setting the example that hard work pays off.

One special person in my life, who has been by my side through thick and thin, is Mark Bradford. He's always there for me, standing in the shadows, showing and giving me his full support. He has never discouraged my dreams and always encouraged me to take the next step, no matter what tomorrow may hold. Mark, I will never be able to thank you enough for all you have done and continue to do, from being my full-time dishwasher to my go-to when I need advice and encouragement; being my support system, never giving up on me; and designing the beautiful floral arrangements in the cookbook. You have all my love and appreciation, just for being you.

When I say it has taken a village to get me where I am today, that is no understatement. The list is endless, but just to name a few: Wayne Esterle, Harriette Miller, Nicole Jacob, my Huntington Hills family, my Lakeside Hills community, Sponge Bob and Jayne Schwartz, my Elliott County school family, and my Old Salem Church family. Thank you from the bottom of my heart.

To my fans, who have been faithful in encouraging me to write a cookbook, this labor of love is for y'all. A big thank-you to my product agent, Paul Leon-hardt, for working so hard to bring me my first cookbook deal.

Thank you to my dear friends, who are like my family, Randy and Samra Evans, for realizing my vision of how I wanted my food to look. Evans Photography of Morehead, Kentucky, you have truly blessed this cookbook with some of the most beautiful food pictures ever.

Lastly, but certainly not least, I couldn't do what I do without my best friend, Lisa Nickell. She is that one friend who doesn't shrink from telling me how it is, whether it's taste-testing a recipe, converting my jumbled thoughts into words, or helping me pick out an outfit. I never have to guess what her opinion is, because she is more than willing to share it with me. We have had more laughs than one person should ever have in one lifetime. She is the epitome of a true friend, always there for the good times and willing to carry you over the finish line during the bad. Sometimes it takes both her and her husband, Charles, to pack me across. Thank you, Charles, for loaning her to me so often. Words are never enough, but thank you, Lisa, from the bottom of my heart for being my friend and providing the words that allow me to share my stories and recipes with so many. Love ya, Sista.

INDEX

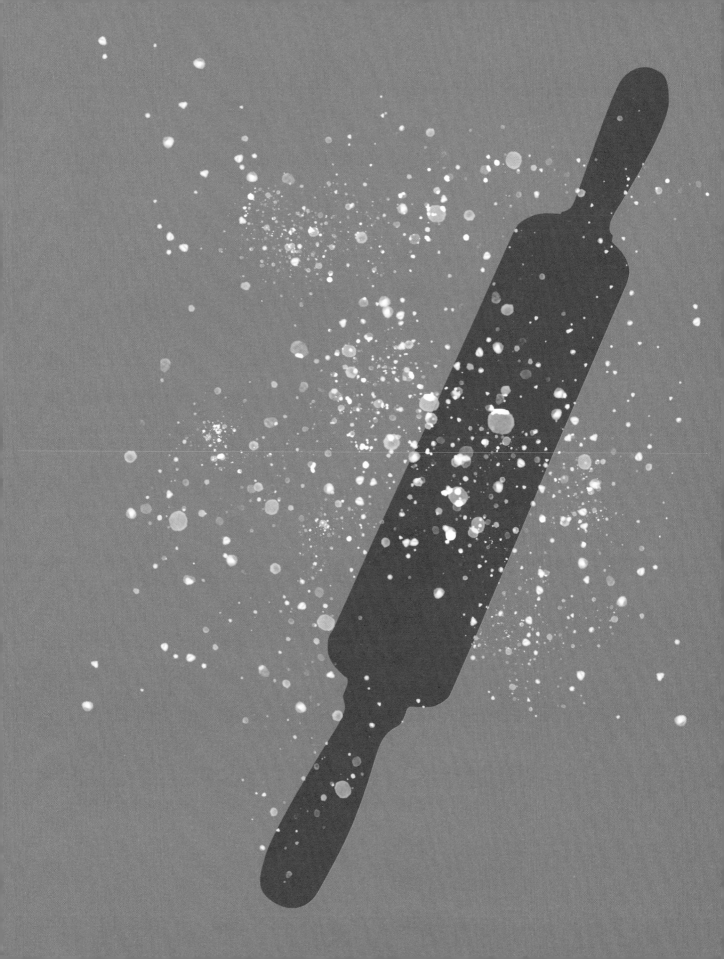

Known for his dazzling fashion, quick quips in the kitchen, and delicious cooking, Lord Honey Chef Jason Smith brings it right back to his granny's kitchen in Kentucky in this cookbook. From humble beginnings as a school-cafeteria cooking manager and caterer, the breakout star of the Food Network went on to win *Holiday Baking Championship*, season 3; *Holiday Baking Championship, Kids vs. Adults* 2016; and the title of *Food Network Star*, season 13.

Smith loves cooking up, right, down, and center, saying, "Honey, if cookin' is a chore, then you ain't been doin' it right." He is currently a television food judge for programs such as *Best Baker in America*, *Worst Bakers in America*, and many other cooking competitions.